EARNING A CRUST
A CENTURY OF THE BAKING TRADE IN WARWICK
(1860s – 1960s)

This image and the cover photograph are of Martin and Ralph Brown in the bakehouse of Brown's Bakery, 41 Albion St, Warwick. The bread rolls featured in the photographs were produced for the Grand Prix, a 240 km race run on 18 September 1949 on a former wartime aerodrome circuit near Leyburn, c. 70 km north-east of Warwick. This was the first national motor race staged in Queensland and, with an estimated crowd of 30,000, catering was understandably a priority. (Both photographs from author's collection. Unknown photographer.)

EARNING A CRUST
A CENTURY OF THE BAKING TRADE IN WARWICK
(1860s – 1960s)

Judith Anderson

EARNING A CRUST: A CENTURY OF THE BAKING TRADE
IN WARWICK (1860s – 1960s)

Published by Judith Anderson
Cansdale St, Yeronga, Queensland, Australia

First edition – April 2021
Revised first edition – October 2021

Copyright © Judith Anderson

This book is copyright.
Apart from any fair dealing for the purposes of private study, research, criticism or review as permitted under the *Copyright Act*, no part may be reproduced by any process without written permission. All rights reserved. Enquiries should be addressed to the author.

ISBN 978-0-646-83043-8

Designed by Six String Design Pty Ltd, Kenmore Hills, Queensland.

CONTENTS

AUTHOR'S NOTE	9
EARNING A CRUST	11
AUSTRALIA'S EARLY FLOUR MILLS AND BAKERIES	14
WARWICK'S FIRST BAKERS	17
Celestino Gobbi Clarkeo and John Jefferson Paul Clarke	21
John Healy	24
Benjamin Ingham	28
Joseph Lane	33
James McDougall	34
West Hamilton McQuaker	35
Joseph and Mrs Stockbridge	38
INTO THE TWENTIETH CENTURY	42
Richard Emil Bochman	42
Martin and Ralph Brown	51
Stanley Cain and Alfred Thorne	61
Clarke and Glasby	65
Lloyd and Henry ('Harry') Crone	67
Daniel Maunsell	70
Louis, Les and Gordon Overstead	73
The Parker Family	78
Henry Tucker and the Tucker Brothers	86
DELIVERY AND DISTRIBUTION	91
TOOLS OF THE TRADE	101
THE CHEMISTRY AND ALCHEMY OF BREAD	112
STAYING OUT OF TROUBLE	119
WARWICK'S FLOUR MILLS	124

WARWICK'S BAKEHOUSES	137
32A King Street	138
149 Palmerin Street (Derby House)	141
41 Albion Street	145
148 Palmerin Street (Elsleys)	150
58 Grafton Street	154
76 Grafton Street	158
Cnr Percy Street and Oak Avenue	161
OUR DAILY BREAD	167
REFLECTIONS	173
RECOMMENDED READING AND RESOURCES	175
ENDNOTES AND REFERENCES	179

For Ralph and Amy Brown

Ralph and Amy Brown and their daughter Judith in 1946. (Photograph from author's collection.)

Ralph, Amy and Judith Brown with the FX at Southport, Gold Coast, 1953.
(Photograph from author's collection.)

AUTHOR'S NOTE

The stimulus for this book came from an unlikely source.

In April 2020, I was contacted by the owner of a 50-2106 Holden utility, the much-loved 'stripey grille' model colloquially referred to as the FX.

In the search for the history of the vehicle, he had followed a trail back through at least six owners in three Australian states, as well as several different engines, evidence of an accident, and a colour change from its original Burnley Cream to light blue. At the end of the search, it appeared that it had been purchased, new, in October 1952 by my father, Ralph Brown, for use in his bakery business in Warwick and had remained there, with other owners, until 1991.

Proof that this was indeed Ralph's ute was more difficult to find. With the number plate and other registration details irretrievably lost and only my imperfect memory and collection of old family photographs to draw on, it became obvious that if I were to help in this search, I would need a much clearer picture of the bakeries and the people who worked in them in the 1950s to see how my family's ute fitted into that picture. This, in turn, drew me further back into Warwick's history, to the city's very first bakers and bakeries and those of the first half of the 20th century. The people I discovered were enterprising, resilient, hard-working and generous but largely unknown and unsung. At the end of the process, I felt that their stories should be told and preserved. This book is the result.

Many bakers, baking families and people with a connection to Warwick responded to my requests for information, stories and photographs and, fortuitously, the months of restricted activity imposed by the COVID-19 pandemic in 2020 meant that they had the time to reflect and respond and I had the time to research and write.

My thanks go to them all, especially Michael Carter for his knowledge of the baking trade and processes; the families and descendants of Richard Bochman, Stanley Cain, Louis Overstead, Fred Parker, Wally Siebuhr, Fred Tanna and Henry Tucker for fact-checking and for sharing their stories and photographs; Ana Gray, Michael Otago, David Owens and Ortrun Zuber-Skerritt for their editorial feedback; Peter Ball, Frank Winters and Janine Nicklin for their publishing and design expertise; and many others for their contributions and encouragement, particularly (in alphabetical order) Penny Campbell Wilson, Matthew Collins, David Glasgow, Mark Halsey, Mavis March, Nola Mikkelsen, Paul Munson, Eric Turner and the hundreds (literally!) of members of the Facebook group, *Lost Faces of Warwick and District*, whose reminiscences have enriched the stories and revived many of my own childhood memories of Christmas hams baked in bread dough, the taste of cream buns, and the incomparable aroma of fresh bread.

The author in 1947. (Photograph from Brown family collection.)

They have all been exceptionally generous in sharing their knowledge, contacts, recollections and records. While every effort has been made to ensure accuracy, in an informal social, family and cultural history such as this, with access to published records severely restricted by the pandemic, there will inevitably be errors and omissions, and for these I apologise. Acknowledgements have been included wherever possible.

Judith Anderson
Brisbane, April 2021

EARNING A CRUST

Bread has been a staple food for centuries, even millennia. However, the word 'bread' in English has taken on a life of its own.

Thanks to Cockney rhyming slang, we have everything from 'bread and cheese' for 'sneeze' to 'loaf of bread' for 'head', and 'brown bread' for 'dead'.

But rhyming slang has also given us 'bread and honey' for 'money'. Shortened to 'bread', it has become a colloquial expression for money throughout the English-speaking world.

From 'bread' it's a very short linguistic step to 'crust' and another enduring expression: 'to earn a crust'.

In Australia, earning a crust as a baker was not possible until commercial bakeries first emerged in the early nineteenth century; in Warwick, it wasn't until the 1860s that the population reached a sufficient size to support a viable bakery business.

The story of the baking trade in Warwick therefore begins around the time of the town's declaration as a municipality in 1861.

The logical end-point for the story was the middle of the twentieth century because, from this time, the large, wood- and gas-fired ovens and the artisanal nature of the baking trade began to disappear. These trends were brought about by changes in retail structures and domestic buying habits (the arrival of supermarkets), dramatic changes in flour milling and distribution, rapid developments in bread science and technology, and the construction of efficient road networks which brought mass-produced, sliced bread within the reach of almost every family.

The overall picture that emerges from those one hundred years is of a trade in which earning a crust required long hours of hard, physical labour in unpleasant conditions and in which success depended not only on hard work, but on inventiveness, business acumen, skill as an artisan, and willingness to collaborate.

What the lives of Warwick's first bakers also reveal is the strength of family and the disproportionate number of men and women in the trade who were genuinely committed to giving back to Warwick, whether by serving in public office or through significant contributions to a wide range of professional and social organisations.

The author has connections to three interrelated Warwick baking families – the Oversteads, the Tuckers and the Browns (see diagram p. 13). As a result, this is a personal story as well as an account of the first century of the baking trade in Warwick.

To see that account and the family story in context, the book begins with background about Australia's and Queensland's early bakeries and flour mills. It then tells the stories of some of the remarkable baking pioneers and others who worked in the trade during Warwick's first century. The book also traces the history of Warwick's flour mills and the successive owners of the large bakehouses known to have existed.

Woven into these stories are broader events that affected all of Australia – immigration, two world wars, and the Great Depression. Another recurring theme is the hope of building a bright and prosperous future through hard work and enterprise.

The book includes a list of some 160 owners, bakers, pastrycooks and carters identified as having worked in the trade in Warwick over the century concerned, as well as sections dealing with bread distribution, the bread-making process, ovens and other essential equipment, the role of various baking associations, and the importance of institutions such as the Bread Research Institute in contributing the science that turned baking into the bread manufacturing industry. Useful sources of further information about Warwick's history are also included and some concluding reflections.

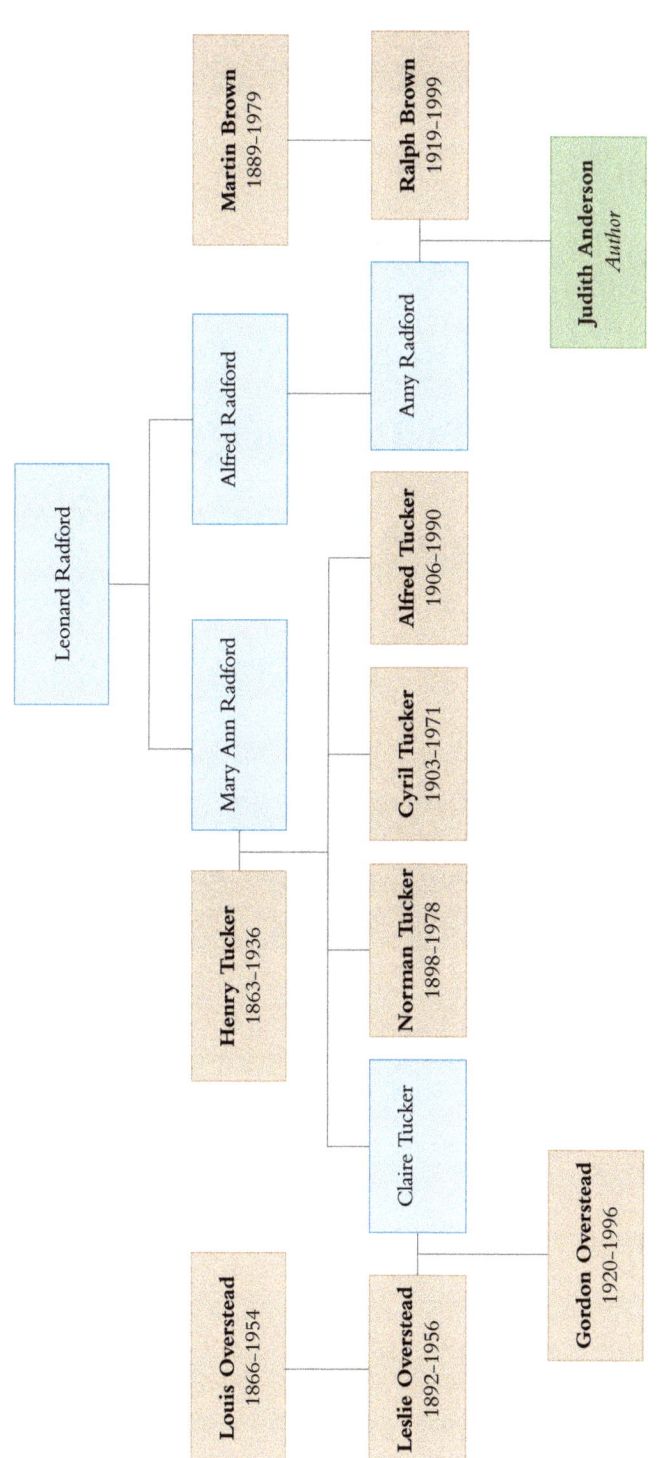

THE OVERSTEADS, TUCKERS AND BROWNS
Only the individuals and relationships relevant to the baking trade are shown in this diagram.

AUSTRALIA'S EARLY FLOUR MILLS AND BAKERIES

For many thousands of years, Australia's Indigenous peoples ground seeds to make bread, but in January 1788, the ships of the First Fleet brought the first wheat as well as some 40 iron hand-mills to the colony.[1] This marked the beginning of flour milling and bread-making as industries in what would become Australia.

As man- and horse-powered mills replaced hand-mills, flour milling quickly spread. By 1809, seven windmills were working in Sydney, and by 1815, the first steam-driven mill had begun operation.

As settlement and agriculture spread beyond Sydney, the number of mills in New South Wales increased sharply from 46 in 1830 to an estimated one hundred by 1840.

Often, the miller was also the baker, but other bakers purchased flour and set up business. In 1821 there were 52 licensed bakers in Sydney.

The same pattern of development was repeated in other settlements. In Brisbane, for example, a windmill was constructed in 1828 to process the wheat and corn crops of the Moreton Bay penal settlement, with a treadmill attached for times when there was no wind.

The 1844 map of Brisbane[2] (p. 16) shows both the windmill (no. 18) and the settlement's only bakery at the time (no. 3), operated by a Mr H. Savary.

Beyond an occasional advertisement for his goods (p. 15) and the incident

**CHRISTMAS CAKES! CHRISTMAS CAKES!
ORNAMENTAL TWELFTH CAKE
TO BE RAFFLED FOR AT
MR. SAVARY'S,
NORTH BRISBANE,**
On THURSDAY, THE 6TH JANUARY NEXT,
A SPLENDID TWELFTH CAKE, warranted to weigh
60 POUNDS!
and of the best quality that can be made in the colony.
Try Brisbane all round,
Its equal is not to be found!

A large supply of CHRISTMAS CAKES, of the very best quality, can be had at the house of the undersigned.

All kinds of Wine and Fancy Biscuits.
Ships supplied with the first and second quality Biscuits, at the shortest notice.
Up-country orders executed with punctuality and dispatch.

The undersigned also takes this opportunity to return his grateful thanks to the public of Moreton Bay for the kind support with which he has been favoured during the four years he has been in business, and hopes that he will continue to obtain the same patronage, which he will endeavour by assiduity and attention to deserve.
HENRY SAVARY.

SAT 25 DEC 1847. P1. MB COURIER

Savary v. Slade.—The sum claimed was £5 17s., being the amount of an account for bread, flour, &c. The defendant had filed a plea that he was not indebted, the goods having been supplied for the use of the deceased Mr. George M. Slade. A good deal of discussion ensued, but eventually the plea was held valid, and the case dismissed.

SAT 6 MAY 1848. P2. MB COURIER

Brisbane windmill, Wickham Terrace, 1840.[3]

reported in *The Moreton Bay Courier* in 1848 (above right), little is known of Mr Savary. However, the court case described illustrates a feature of the baking trade which would become a constant as the industry developed – disagreements and disputes with customers, suppliers, employees' unions and the government about matters ranging from regulations, hours of work and wages, to the price and quality of bread and flour. It was a tough trade.

By the 1850s, advertisements like those below began to appear in *The Moreton Bay Courier* in Brisbane for bakeries such as those established by Mr J.S. Good in Edward St and by William Warren in South Brisbane.

NOTICE.

J. S. GOOD, late of Ipswich, most respectfully begs to apprise the Inhabitants of Brisbane that he has now opened a Confectioner's and Bakery Establishment in Edward-street, three doors from Mr. Smith's Tinware Factory, where he will be most happy to execute any orders that he may be favoured with in the Baking and Confectionery business. Picknicks attended to on the shortest notice, and Bride-Cakes, &c., supplied.

☞ Dinners carefully baked every day.—On Sundays the shop will be open for that purpose from 11 A.M. until 1 P.M.

SAT 6 JUL 1850. P1. MB COURIER

**NEW BAKERY ESTABLISHMENT,
RUSSELL STREET, SOUTH BRISBANE.**

THE undersigned has much pleasure in notifying to the public, that in connection with his Grocery, Wine, and Spirit Store, he intends to carry on the business of a Baker; and has engaged a master baker for the purpose.

The advertiser trusts that the bread from his Establishment will be found to be of the best quality, and families on making timely arrangements may also have dinners baked.
WILLIAM WARREN,
Russell-street, South Brisbane

SAT 15 DEC 1855. P3. MB COURIER

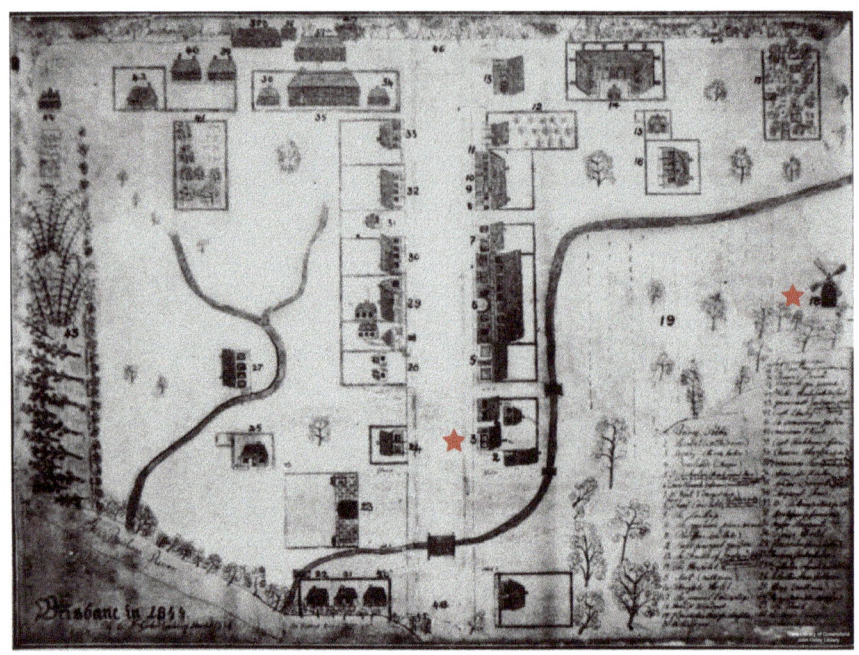

Map of Brisbane, 1844.

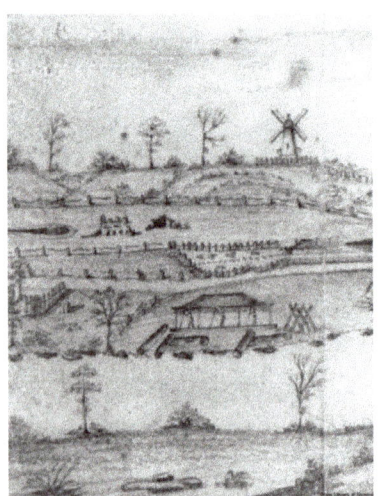

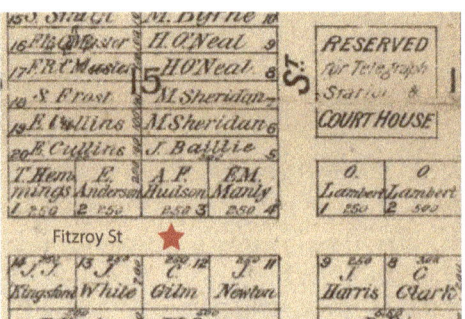

Location of Gilm's bakery in Fitzroy St on 1879 plan of the town of Warwick.[4] (State Library of Queensland.)

Pencil sketch of the Moreton Bay Settlement drawn from South Brisbane, attributed to Henry W. Boucher Bowerman, c. 1835.
(Image from collection of State Library of Queensland.)

WARWICK'S FIRST BAKERS

Although Warwick town had been gazetted in 1849, and the first sales of allotments took place in 1850, the only mention of bakers, bakeries or confectioners in Thomas Hall's history of early Warwick is: 'In Fitzroy Street, facing the Queen's Hotel, Mr Charles Gilm, the German baker, had a well-stocked General Store, where almost anything could be purchased for cash'.[5]

Gilm migrated from Fellbach (near Stuttgart) in Germany on the ship *Helene* in 1855, possibly as a result of successful recruitment by Queensland immigration agents who operated during the period from 1852 to 1855. He was 45 when he arrived and by 8 September 1857, had purchased Allotment 12 in Section 15 on Fitzroy St, near the corner with Albion St. (See street plan p. 16.)

He was 'naturalised'[6] in August 1858 and was recorded in Warwick business registers until 1877. While he was referred to by Hall as a baker, Gilm is more often described as a storekeeper, and advertisements such as the 1873 Requisition in the *Warwick Examiner and Times* (p. 18) indicate that he played a prominent role in civic life in Warwick until 1879 when he retired, wound up his business, and returned to Europe.

No other bakers have been found in directories or other records in the 1850s. This is possibly because the population of Warwick was still small (see table on p. 18), but also because the early hotels and inns would have produced their

REQUISITION.

To Mr. CHARLES COLAS.

WE, the undersigned Ratepayers of Warwick, request that you will allow yourself to be Nominated as a candidate to fill the vacancy caused by the resignation of Alderman Balls. In the event of your doing so, we will do all in our power to ensure your return.

Warwick, 4th November, 1873.

John Ferguson, Blacksmith, Fitzroy-street.
G. W. Chavasse, Fruiterer, do
Charles Gilm, Storekeeper, do
David Clarke, Druggist, do
William Collins, Butcher, do
Christopher Roggenkamp, Photographer, Albion-street.
William Zwoerner, Carpenter, Albion-street.
Albert Frank, Tailor, do
George Seabrook, Butcher, Palmerin-street.
C. G. Clarke, Baker, do
W. Sparks, Tailor, do
C. Barth, Saddler, do
Jacob Horwitz, Storekeeper, do
John S. Roxton, Watchmaker, do
G. I. Wickham, Corn Chandler, do
James Morgan, Newspaper Proprietor, Victoria-street.
P. Hoffman, Saddler, Victoria-street.
R. A. Cowton, Newspaper Proprietor, Albion-street.

SAT 8 NOV 1873. P3. WET

Pioneer Bakery and General Store,
STANNUM.

D. GRIGG

BEGS to announce to his friends and the residents of the TIN MINES, that he has

REMOVED

TO HIS

NEW PREMISES,

Where he will always have on hand a Large and Varied STOCK of GOODS, which are offered at

The Lowest Cash Prices.

The BAKERY is also enlarged, and every attention paid to the wants of customers.

☞ TIN ORE BOUGHT AT HIGHEST CASH PRICE.   584

SAT 27 JUL 1872. P3. WET

RETIRING FROM BUSINESS !!

LEAVING FOR EUROPE.

IMPORTANT SALE
OF
GENERAL GOODS, TOOLS,
AND ARTICLES
Suitable for Shoemakers, Saddlers, Builders, Cabinetmakers, Stonemasons, Bricklayers, Sawyers, and Fencers, &c., &c.

CHAS. GILM,

HAVING sold his premises, and decided to leave Warwick, is now compelled to WIND UP HIS BUSINESS with as little delay as possible. He therefore offers the Whole of his Stock of

General Groceries
Ironmongery
Fancy Goods, &c.

AT AND UNDER COST PRICE

As it is necessary for him to Wind Up quickly. As all Accounts are closed, the terms are

Cash Only!

CHARLES GILM,

General Storekeeper,
FITZROY-STREET, WARWICK.
(Opposite Mr. Hubert's Auction Mart.)

THU 17 APR 1879. P1. WATC

POPULATION OF WARWICK
1857   1362
1871   2469
1881   3602
1891   3402
1902   3838
1911   5562
1921   6091
1933   6664
1947   7129
1954   9151
1961   9843
1991   10624
2001   12011
2006   13340

own bread, families on the surrounding farms and in the growing town would have baked bread in the home, and no flour was produced locally until 1861.

However, by the mid-1860s, commercial bakers had begun to appear. As the wheat and wool industries developed and the railway was extended from Ipswich to Warwick in 1871, the size of the town increased. (In the decade between 1871 and 1881, the population grew by 38 per cent.)

This growth was boosted by the great alluvial tin rush in the nearby town of Stanthorpe which produced a virtual stampede of arrivals on horseback and on foot, as well as by coach. According to a report in the *Warwick Examiner and Times* on 2 March 1872, Cobb and Co. even ran express services twice a day from the railway terminus in Warwick to Stanthorpe, with passengers clinging precariously to every available part of the coach.

Writing as 'Gooragooby' in the *Warwick Daily News* in 1934, Donald McInnes (p. 177) reported that, at the time of the rush, no fewer than seven bakers had set up business in Stanthorpe – as well as three cordial manufacturers, three chemists, four blacksmiths, five saddlers, six bootmakers, 20 carpenters, 20 store-keepers, and (perhaps not surprisingly) 25 hotel-keepers.[7]

The tin rush was not confined to Stanthorpe; there were also finds south of the Queensland border in Stannum,[a] near Tenterfield, and it, too, had its baker entrepreneurs. Daniel Grigg's Pioneer Bakery and General Store not only provided bread and a variety of goods for the residents and tin miners but purchased tin ore – for cash.[8]

Records have been found of seven bakers who operated in Warwick during the 1870s.

James McDougall was first listed as operating in Palmerin St in the 1868 directory, and three additional confectioners and bakers appeared in the 1874 edition (Benjamin Ingham, Mrs Stockbridge, and G.C. Clarke). McQuaker and Co. advertised for the first time in June 1875 and are also listed in the 1877 directory; Joseph Lane is first mentioned in an advertisement in the *Warwick Examiner and Times* in the same year. While John Healy's principal business was as a grocer, his obituary refers to his carrying on 'the business of baker, etc.' and records of several young bakers who arrived in Warwick in the late 19th century name Healy as their employer.

---

a   The names of both Stanthorpe and Stannum are derived from the Latin word for 'tin' – stannum.

The Border Bakery was one of the seven bakeries operating in Stanthorpe in the 1870s. Bread was a staple of the tin miner's diet and the wheaten loaf or damper, made when brewer's yeast could not be procured, went well with black tea, salted meat and potatoes. Ground maize, boiled rice and other things were added to the bread which was later stamped with its maker's initials. A two-pound loaf sold in Stanthorpe for about sixpence in 1873. (Digitised copy of a damaged print from William Boag Photograph Albums 1870-1880 John Oxley Library, State Library of Queensland. Description supplied with photograph.)

The seven stories which follow have been pieced together from tantalisingly scant records. The advertisements they placed in Warwick's early newspapers,[b] business directories, newspaper reports, electoral rolls, genealogy websites such as Ancestry.com, government registers of births death and marriages, cemetery records, Queensland State Library and State Archives, books and records held by the Warwick Library and Warwick Historical Society, and sites such as the National Library of Australia's *Trove* website have all been used to breathe life into the bare facts.

The stories of Clarkeo, Healy, Ingham, Lane, McDougall, McQuaker and the Stockbridges are presented in alphabetical order.

---

b   The first newspaper established in Warwick was the *Warwick Argus and Tenterfield Chronicle (WATC)* which began publication in November 1864 and continued until 21 August 1879 when it was renamed the *Warwick Argus (WA)*. It continued publication until 1919. The *Warwick Examiner and Times (WET)* began operation in competition with the *Chronicle* in 1867 and it, too, continued until 1919 when the *Warwick Daily News (WDN)* became the town's only newspaper. Before 1864, the closest local news source was the *Darling Downs Gazette* published from 1858 to 1922 in Drayton and Toowoomba.
Unless otherwise identified, all newspaper clippings included in this book are from the *Warwick Daily News*.

Celestino Gobbi Clarkeo and John Jefferson Paul Clarke

With rare exceptions, Celestino Gobbi Clarkeo was known to the people of Warwick simply as 'C.G.'. Even the announcement of his death in the *Warwick Examiner and Times* on 9 March 1890 referred to him only by his initials.

Despite his unusual name, records are not easily traced because his given name has been recorded variously as Celestino, Celestina, Celeste and Celestial, and his middle name as Gobby, Gobbi, and Gobi. Even his family name appears as Clarke, Clarkes and Clarkeo in different records.

The first definitive record found is of his marriage[9] in 1866 to Charlotte Langford in the Blue Mountains village of Hartley (near Lithgow, NSW), followed by an 1867 record of being granted a publican's license.

Name.	Situation.	Sign of House.
HARTLEY DISTRICT.		
Gobby Celestial	Bell's Line of Road and Darling Causeway.	Junction Inn

NEW SOUTH WALES GOVERNMENT GAZETTE, 13 AUG 1867, ISSUE NO. 136 (SUPPLEMENT), P.1898

C.G.'s trail becomes easier to trace once the first of the couple's seven children, John Jefferson Paul Clarke, is born the year after their marriage, followed by their first daughter, Catherine Charlotte in 1869. At some point after Catherine's birth, the family evidently relocated to Warwick because the births of the subsequent four children all appear in Queensland birth records – Charles Henry (aka Henry Carlo) in 1873, Sarah Jane in 1874, Emily (Evelyn) Maude in 1877, Prosper Edgar in 1880 and Charlotte Nina in 1885.

In addition, Clarke's name appears in the 1874 Warwick business directory and the report (p. 22) in the *Warwick Argus and Tenterfield Chronicle* in May 1874 indicates that, by then, C.G. had established his business in Palmerin St. Donald McInnes[10] also refers to the bakery, locating it on the southern side of the building owned by Prussong, the German tobacconist, and later by Teitzel. (See photograph p. 79.)

It appears that, within the next two years, Clarke was operating the bakery at 41 Albion St. The evidence for this comes from an unexpected source – the photographic record of the flood of January 1887, one of the most disastrous

View of Albion St looking north from near the corner of Fitzroy St during the 1887 flood, showing C.G. Clarkeo's confectionery business on the left and the then Post and Telegraph Office and Lands Office on the right. (Image sourced from Picture Queensland, State Library of Queensland.)

We were shown yesterday two loaves of bread from the bakery of Mr. C. G. Clarke, of Palmerin-street, one made from the finest silk dressed Adelaide, the other from flour manufactured in Toowoomba, from wheat grown on Farm Creek, and, although we consider ourselves very fair judges in the matter, we were puzzled to tell " tother from which ;" in taste, color, and quality we really could see no difference.

THU 14 MAY 1874. P2. WATC

'Silk dressed Adelaide' is a South Australian flour which was generally viewed as superior to flour produced in Queensland at the time.

Pure Bread.   Pure Bread.
C. G. CLARKEO,
Fancy Bread and Biscuit Maker,
Fitzroy-street, Warwick.

BEGS to intimate to his many customers and the Public generally that his Fancy Bread and Biscuit Baking business is still carried on at the Bakery at the above address. Nothing but the best material used.
C. J. Clarkeo has taken Three First Prize for best bread at the various Exhibitions.

SAT 7 SEP 1889. P6. WET

in Warwick's history.[11] One of the few surviving photographs from the event is of Albion St, near the intersection with Fitzroy St, clearly showing the sign 'Confectioner' on the awning of the shop at 41 Albion St (see above). That this was C.G.'s shop is corroborated by a detailed report of the flood naming his shop as one of those inundated.[12]

By September 1889, Clarkeo was still in business, advertising his 'pure bread' and promoting his success in various exhibitions (see advertisement above). As this mentions Fitzroy St as the address of the bakery, Clarkeo had evidently moved at some point before this date, perhaps prompted by the flooding of his business in 1887. However, the location of the Fitzroy St bakery has not yet been identified.

Although C.G. was still advertising his business, it is clear that his health was in decline by this time because the notice of his death early the following year[13] records that he had been ill for six months. He was aged 49 when he died from 'inflammation of the heart' on 9 March 1890.

DEATH.

CLARKEO.—On Sunday last, March 9, at his residence, Fitzroy-street, Warwick, after a six months' illness, from inflammation of the heart, C. G. Clarkeo, baker, aged 49 years.

WED 12 MAR 1890. P2. WET

SUDDEN DEATH.

Our readers will regret to learn that Mr. John Clarke, baker, of Fitzroy-street, died suddenly at his residence last night at a quarter to 11. The deceased, who was a young man, was seized with a fit on Thursday, but it was not expected that his end was so near. General sympathy, we feel sure, will be extended to the widow in her sad bereavement. The funeral is announced to take place to-morrow at 1·30 p.m.

SAT 20 JAN 1900. P7. WET

Photographs courtesy of Eric Turner.

His eldest son, John, had followed his father into the trade and continued to work as a baker until he also died,[14] suddenly and unexpectedly, on 19 January 1900 at the age of just 32.[c] In total, father and son had maintained the family baking business in Warwick for a quarter of a century.

Both C.G. and his son are buried in the Catholic section of the Warwick Cemetery, as are several other Clarke children and C.G.'s wife Charlotte who remained in Warwick until her death on 2 August 1917.

From his given names, it can be assumed that C.G.'s mother was of Italian heritage, but why he adopted an Italian version of his English family name is not known.

---

c   While the cause of John Clarke's death is not known, bakers often suffered from 'Baker's Asthma', a disease caused by inhaling flour dust and other substances commonly found in bakeries such as amylase enzymes used as bread improver.

John Healy

(From group photograph of founding members of the Warwick Municipal Council, 1901. Unidentified photographer. State Library of Queensland.)

The baker who arguably has the most lasting presence in the Warwick community is Irishman, John Healy, who was to become known as 'the father' of the Town Hall clock.

Born in County Limerick, Healy married Catherine (Kate) Perdeaux in April 1860 and they migrated to Australia on the *Conway*, arriving on 1 December 1862. They made their way to Warwick where their first son, Joseph Michael, was born in 1864.

Their second son, John Edward James, was born in 1869, by which stage Healy was well on his way to establishing his baking and grocery business in Guy St, Warwick, going on to stand successfully for election as an alderman. He served continuously on the local Council[15] for 33 years from 1882, including two terms as Mayor.

When he died on 19 December 1918, aged 84, the obituaries published in newspapers throughout the region showed clearly that he was both greatly respected and regarded with great affection. The tribute published the day after his death in the *Warwick Examiner and Times* tells his story in detail and is reproduced in full on the next page.

DEATH OF MR JOHN HEALY
End of a long life of usefulness

When the sad news spread on Thursday that Mr John Healy, of Guy-street, had passed away at 2.30 that afternoon there were universal expressions of deep regret. Mr Healy had been ailing for about two or three years past, but he kept up wonderfully well, and it was only about two or three weeks ago that he finally took to his bed. His death, therefore, was not unexpected, but the removal of one who had been so long identified with the business, municipal and religious life of the town caused a feeling of genuine sorrow in every heart.

Aged 84 years, Mr Healy was born in County Limerick, Ireland, and was a son of Mr J.H.M. Healy, a close relation of the Home Rule member of that name. He was educated at the State school at Coolcappa, Ireland, and arrived in Queensland in 1862 with Mrs Healy, whom he had married two years previously in the old land. In 1863 he settled in Warwick and entered into business here. For over 40 years of that period he carried on the business of baker, etc., in his Guy-street shop.

Mr Healy always had an ambition to enter into municipal life, and in 1882 he became a member of the then Warwick Municipal Council. He had the unique record of having been an alderman for 33 years continuously. Though often opposed at the polls he was never defeated for he had hundreds of friends who, under no circumstances, would vote against John Healy.

Not only was he the father of the council, but he was also the 'father of the clock'. Mr Healy's reminiscences of the fight he made to have the present Town Hall clock inserted in the Town Hall tower were most interesting. To-day his photograph hangs in the Council Chambers with a clock face inset at one corner.

Failing health compelled him to retire in January 1915. He was twice Mayor of the town – in 1891 and in 1911. Mr Healy's imperturbable good nature, his obvious sincerity, and his desire to fairly serve the ratepayers won for him the admiration of his brother aldermen in no matter what council he sat. Even during the stirring municipal times of 1911, when feeling at times ran high, Mayor Healy was seldom reproached, and his good-natured comments raised many a laugh when the tension appeared to be approaching breaking point. When he finally retired in 1915 all the aldermen expressed their deep sense of appreciation of his services, and the townspeople later made him a public presentation.

The late Mr Healy took a deep interest in the affairs of the Warwick branch of the Hibernian and Australasian Catholic Benefit Society; indeed, it was largely due to his efforts that the branch was established in 1882. Mr Healy secured thirteen foundation members, obtained 10s each from them, and from that small beginning the society has grown, to its present strength today. He served a term as president, and was a trustee right up to the time of his death.

He was a devout member of the Roman Catholic Church and was, perhaps, its leading layman. He very largely assisted, also, in the establishment here of the Warwick Convent and the Christian Brothers' College. Indeed, there was no church function in which he was not a valued worker. As a Justice of the Peace and a Licensing Justice he did fine work when those offices possessed more prestige than they do to-day. His name is writ large in Warwick's history, and his many achievements in a long and useful life will not soon be forgotten.

He is survived by his widow and one son – Mr J.E. Healy. The eldest son – Mr Joseph Healy – passed away some considerable time ago, and a grandson, Bombardier Thomas Healy, made the supreme sacrifice in France. The funeral, which took place yesterday afternoon to St Mary's Church and thence to the Warwick cemetery was exceptionally largely attended. Included in the cortege were members of the Hibernian Society and also many country people who came in to pay their last respects to the departed. The service at the graveside was conducted by Father Potter, assisted by Father Richard McNamara, who is a native of Warwick.

Warwick Examiner and Times, 20 December 1918

Warwick Town Hall in 1897 after the installation of the clock c. 1892. (Queensland State Archives.)

Reports of Council meetings show that Healy deserved to be known as the father of the clock because it was only through his determination that the clock was installed.

He also gave dedicated service to the Catholic Church, and his commitment to the Warwick Hibernian Society was acknowledged by a piped lament at the society's Boxing Day luncheon, just a week after his death. His wife, Kate, died on 3 May 1923.

A Merry Christmas and a Happy New Year to All.

JOHN HEALY,

IN returning thanks for the liberal patronage he has received during the last four years, would draw special attention to his very Large and Well-Assorted Stock of

GROCERIES & OILMEN'S STORES,

Specially selected for this Festive Season, at prices as Low as the Largest House in the Trade. The Public will be satisfied by calling at his Store in Guy-street.
JOHN HEALY.

N.B.—The BEST BREAD in Warwick always on hand. 1050

SAT 24 DEC 1881. P3. WA

Oilmen's stores were originally goods preserved in oil. Oilmen later diversified into salted and dried products, preserves and spices.

Both John Healy and his wife Catherine (Kate) are buried in the same grave as their first son, Joseph Michael, their daughter-in-law Ellen, and four of their grandchildren – Geraldine, Josephine, Leonard and Frank. The grave is in the Old Roman Catholic section of the Warwick Cemetery. (Photograph courtesy of Eric Turner.)

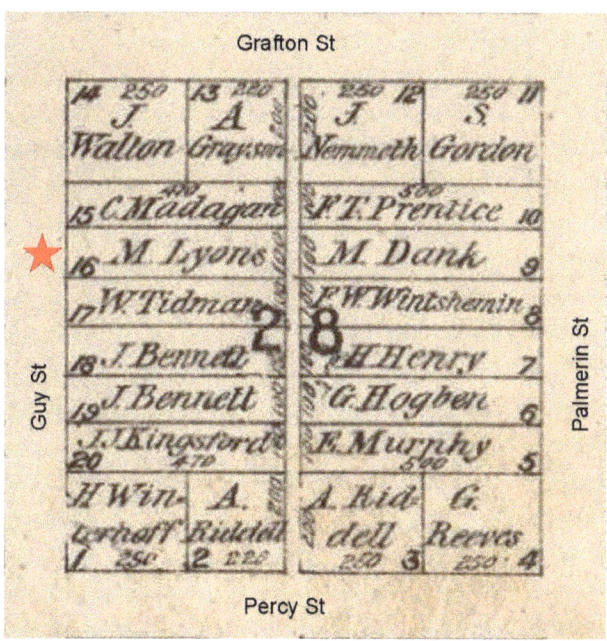

An 1884 advertisement[16] for the sale of 'Mr Healy's Bakery Establishment' in Guy St was described as Allotment 16 of Section 28, with access to the lane at the back of the allotment (Acacia Ave in 2020). (State Library of Queensland. See Endnote 4.)

Benjamin Ingham

Despite his seemingly British name, Benjamin Ingham (according to 'Gooragooby'[17]) was one of the so-called 'Celestials' (Chinese migrants) who established businesses in Warwick in the 1860s.

In addition to the description by 'Gooragooby', there is evidence of Ingham's Chinese origin in the Certificate of Naturalisation issued by Queensland's second governor, Samuel Wensley Blackall, on 8 November 1869,[18] in the Oath of Allegiance signed in Chinese characters on the same date,[19] and in the newspaper report of Ingham's death.

The Certificate of Naturalisation also identifies him as a 45-year-old native of Amoy and as a baker and storekeeper who had been resident in Warwick for 'three years and six months'.

It appears that his date of arrival in the district may have been much earlier because the report of his death in August 1883 mentions that he had been a resident for 'twenty-five years'. This would make his arrival in Warwick 1859 and suggests that he may have been one of the thousands of Chinese indentured labourers who were brought to Australia to work as shepherds for private landholders when transportation of convicts ceased.[d]

Whatever his actual date of arrival, his bakery in Warwick's Albion St was listed in the Warwick business directory in 1874 and, in February 1876, the *Warwick Examiner and Times* announced that his bread had won a special prize at the 10th annual show of the Eastern Downs Horticultural and Agricultural Association held at the Warwick Town Hall. The prize donors, Horwitz and Co., were the owners of Warwick's Steam Flour Mill. (See p. 126.)

Tea. Tea. Tea.
J. SMITH
BEGS to inform his friends and the public of Warwick, that he has OPENED as a
GROCERY & GENERAL STORE,
The premises lately occupied by Mr. F. Jones, in Dragon-street, and hopes by civility and strict attention to business, to receive a share of public patronage.
Every Article of the Best Quality, and at Lowest Prices.
The BEST TEA in Warwick, 2s 6d per lb.
N.B. — Agent for INGHAM'S BREAD, which is delivered daily.   399

SAT 28 APR 1877. P3. WET

---

d   The opening of Chinese ports such as Amoy to foreign trade in the 1850s facilitated the import of indentured labour. Between 1848 and 1853, over 3,000 Chinese workers on labour contracts arrived in Australia, principally from the northern Chinese province of Fujian, for employment in regional New South Wales (then including Victoria and Queensland). Some stayed only for the term of their contracts before returning to China; others remained, married and established businesses and families.

Certificate of Naturalization

By His Excellency Samuel Wensley Blackall, Esquire Governor and Commander in Chief of the Colony of Queensland and its Dependencies.

Whereas a memorial has been presented to me by Benjamin Ingham, setting forth that he is a Baker and Storekeeper resident at Warwick in the Colony of Queensland, and that he is a Native of Amoy in China, that he has been resident at Warwick in the Colony aforesaid for a period of three years and six months, that he is forty-five years of age, that he is married, and that he is desirous of becoming a Naturalized British Subject within the meaning of the Act 31 Victoria N°. 28 entitled "An Act to consolidate and amend the Laws relating to aliens" and praying that I, the said Governor, would grant him a Certificate in pursuance of the aforesaid Act, whereby he may obtain the rights and capacities of a Natural born British Subject. Now therefore I the said Samuel Wensley Blackall, in pursuance of the authority in me vested as Governor of the said Colony, by the aforesaid Act do hereby grant unto the aforesaid Benjamin Ingham (on his taking the oath prescribed by law) all the rights and capacities within the said Colony of Queensland of a Natural born British Subject except the capacity of being a member of either the Executive or Legislative Council, or of the Legislative Assembly of the said Colony.

Given under my Hand and Seal at Government House Brisbane this eighth day of November in the year of Our Lord One Thousand Eight Hundred and Sixty-nine.

By His Excellency's Command
A.H. Palmer

Saml Blackall
Gov.

BAKERS.
Clarke, G. C.
Ingham, B.
McDougall, J.
Stockbridge, Mrs.

PUGH'S ALMANAC AND QUEENSLAND DIRECTORY 1874

Special Prize the Gift of Messrs. Horwitz & Co., for the best 6 two-pound loaves of Bread made from Flour grown and gristed on the Downs, £1 1s. — B. Ingham.

SAT 12 FEB 1876. P2. WET

896a

OATH TO BE TAKEN BY A PERSON OBTAINING A CERTIFICATE OF NATURALIZATION.

I, Benjamin Ingham of the Town of Warwick (Asiatic) do sincerely promise and swear, that I will be faithful and bear true allegiance to Her Majesty Queen Victoria, as lawful Sovereign of the United Kingdom of Great Britain and Ireland, and of this Colony of Queensland, dependent on, and belonging to, the said United Kingdom; and that I will defend her to the utmost of my power against all traitorous conspiracies and attempts whatever which shall be made against Her Person, Crown, and Dignity; and that I will do my utmost endeavor to make known to Her Majesty, Her Heirs and Successors, all treasons and traitorous conspiracies and attempts which I shall know to be against Her or any of them.

So Help me God.

(Signature of Benjamin Ingham)

Sworn and subscribed before me at Warwick this twenty-fifth day of November 1869.

The 1877 edition of the directory indicates that Ingham continued to operate at the same location in Albion St and advertisements reveal that, by that date, his bread was available through agents such as J. Smith's grocery and general store. (See p. 28.)

Ingham's Certificate of Naturalisation also mentions that he was married. His wife was Mary Miller who had arrived in Queensland from Edinburgh in 1863 on the *Costa Eden*. It is not known why she went to Warwick, but a newspaper announcement[20] records that she married Ingham there on 9 March 1866. According to government birth records, their first son, Benjamin Joseph, was born in Warwick in January the following year and two other sons followed – Gilbert and Charles.

The *Warwick Examiner and Times* reported Ingham's death in August 1883 and he is buried in the old Church of England section of the Warwick cemetery. There is no gravestone.

> AN OLD resident of Warwick died on Thursday night last, after a lingering illness. This was Mr. B. Ingham, who for several years carried on the business of a baker in Albion-street. Mr. Ingham was a Chinaman, but many years ago joined the Anglican Church and was married in St. Mark's by the Ven. Archdeacon Glennie. Mr. Ingham leaves a widow and several children. He has been a resident of Warwick about twenty-five years.

SAT 11 AUG 1883. P2. WET

Women and children heading towards buildings at the Dunwich Benevolent Asylum, Queensland, c. 1900. (Photo courtesy John Oxley Library, State Library of Queensland Neg No: 16716.)

According to details on her medical and death record at the Dunwich Benevolent Asylum,[21] Mary worked as a domestic servant after her husband's death, including two years for a Mr Clark in Rockhampton, but in the early 1890s was admitted to hospital in Warwick with 'senile decay'. She was transferred to the Benevolent Asylum in Dunwich[e] (Goompi) on North Stradbroke Island (Minjerribah) in 1893 and spent the last decade of her life there, dying from cardiac failure on 12 June 1903 at the age of 69. She is buried in an unmarked grave in the Asylum cemetery.

A wall and plaque have been erected at Dunwich Cemetery in memory of the patients and staff in unmarked graves.

> **THE DUNWICH BENEVOLENT ASYLUM MEMORIAL WALL**
>
> Dedicated to the memory of the many patients and staff who lie at rest in unmarked graves in this cemetery.
>
> This memorial was erected by Consolidated Rutile Limited from hand-made bricks obtained from parts of the laundry and power house of the institution which operated at Dunwich, North Stradbroke Island, from 1866 until 1946 when the inmates were transferred to the Eventide Home at Sandgate, Brisbane.
>
> February 1988

The Asylum records also reveal that, at the time of his mother's death, Charles had been committed to the Toowoomba Lunatic Asylum by the age of 21, while Benjamin Joseph worked as a barman at Brisbane's Treasury Hotel and Gilbert followed his father into the baking trade.

---

e Until the emergence of benevolent societies in regional centres and the consequent development of homes for the aged and infirm, the government facility on Dunwich was the only available facility for Queenslanders. The first benevolent home in Warwick (The Mill House) opened in October 1915.

Joseph Lane

Joseph Lane has been elusive. His name appeared alongside McDougall, Ingham and McQuaker in the April 1877 advertisement below left in the *Warwick Examiner and Times* advising of an increase in the price of bread. This indicates that he was operating as an independent master baker in Warwick, but the only other record found is of R. Hackett taking over his Grafton St bakery in December of that year. It is not known where Hackett's previous premises were located.

Notice.

IN consequence of the GREAT RISE in the PRICE of FLOUR we are compelled to RISE the PRICE of BREAD to Sixpence per 2lb Loaf from and after May 1st.
JAMES M'DOUGALL.
B. INGHAM.
M'QUAKER & CO.
JOSEPH LANE.

427

SAT 28 APR 1877. P3. WET

NOTICE! NOTICE!!

Removal! Removal!!

R. HACKETT

BEGS to inform his customers and the public generally, that he has REMOVED to those premises in

Grafton-street

(Lately occupied by Mr. Joseph Lane), where he still intends carrying on his Bakery Business, and his customers may rely on getting

Good Bread and Full Weight.

R. HACKETT,
873   Grafton-st., Warwick.

THU 20 DEC 1877. P5. WATC

James McDougall

James McDougall emerges from newspaper records as an enterprising businessman who saw opportunities in the rapidly developing township of Warwick. It is not known when he opened his business, but an advertisement in the *Warwick Examiner and Times* in September 1870 advised the public that his Warwick Bakery and Refreshments Rooms had transferred to a Mr N.T. Rose. Later advertisements in the same newspaper indicate that, within 18 months, McDougall had established a new bakery and general store in Palmerin St and, by June 1872, had offered his Albert St bakery and house for lease or sale. His business was still listed in Palmerin St in the 1877 directory, but no other reports of his time in Warwick have been found.

West Hamilton McQuaker

McQuaker and Co. was established as a business in Warwick in 1875 by West Hamilton McQuaker, one of the eight children of William and Elizabeth McQuaker of Ayrshire, Scotland.

Born c. 1833, by the time of the 1850 census in Scotland, McQuaker is listed as a 17-year-old baker. It is not known when or why he migrated to Australia, but the death of his father in 1851 may have been a factor and there were also strong incentives offered at that time for skilled tradesmen to migrate. In any event, he evidently decided to migrate because the next mention of him is on 7 February 1862 when *The Courier* in Brisbane announces his marriage to another Scottish immigrant, Mary Souter (née Sutherland). She was the widow of John Souter and some 10 years older than McQuaker.

> **MARRIAGE.**
> On the 4th Instant, by the Rev. C. Ogg, West Hamilton M'Quaker, fourth son of the late William M'Quaker, Esq., of Ayrshire, Scotland, to Mary, second daughter of the late Donald Sutherland, Esq., of Sutherlandshire, Scotland, and relict of the late John Souter.

FRI 7 FEB 1862. P2. THE COURIER

McQuaker continued in the baking trade, next being mentioned in a newspaper report in April 1871 when he appeared in the Brisbane Police Court, charged with having no scales in his bakery shop to weigh bread. While the Inspector of Weights and Measures zealously pursued the case, it was dismissed by the Bench.[22]

The McQuakers did not have any children and shortly after their 10th wedding anniversary, in June 1872, Mary died. McQuaker was still not yet 40 and two years later married Fanny Graham, in September 1874.

It appears from advertisements in 1875 and 1876, and from a newspaper report in December 1876 describing him as a 'baker and storekeeper in Stanthorpe'[23] that he and Fanny made a fresh start, moving to the Darling Downs and setting up business in both Warwick and Stanthorpe.

The building in which he established his Palmerin St business in Warwick in June 1875 was owned by German-born tobaconnist, Theodor Prussong, and had opened only a month beforehand. Prussong had first operated a 'cigar divan' business in Albion St in May 1869 but relocated within four months to the western side of Palmerin St before building and opening his new premises, 'The Old Divan', on the eastern side of the street in May 1875. McQuaker became a tenant of the new building just a month later.[f]

Whether or not bread was baked on the premises is not known, but McQuaker ran a successful business until September 1881 when it was taken over by Robert Burnett.[24]

From the late 1880s, McQuaker became increasingly identified with the Stanthorpe community. In 1891, he wrote a passionate Letter to the Editor of the *Warwick Argus* in support of the quality of locally produced flour (p. 37).

In 1893, he won first prize for flour in the Stanthorpe Show 'with a splendid example which was equal to the best Adelaide, and which, we believe, came from the mills of Messrs Barnes, Archibald and Co.'[25] and by 1901, had himself become a judge of flour, meal and bread for the 33rd annual exhibition of the Eastern Downs Horticultural and Agricultural Association – the Warwick Show.[26]

> **NEW BAKERY,**
> Palmerin-street, in Pruesong's New Buildings.
>
> ## McQUAKER & CO.
> BEG to inform the public of Warwick and district, that they have commenced the
>
> **BAKERY BUSINESS**
>
> In those centrally situated and New Premises as above, and would inform them that it will be their determination by supplying the BEST BREAD to merit a share of public patronage. They will also make daily every description of
> **PASTRY**
> **BISCUITS, and**
> **CONFECTIONERY.**
>
> Orders punctually obeyed, and Customers served with regularity.
>
> **Orders received from This Day, the 26th inst.**

SAT 26 JUN 1875. P2. WET

> **NOTICE.**
>
> ## ROBERT BURNETT
> BEGS to notify to his Friends and the General Public that on the
>
> **1st OF OCTOBER NEXT,**
>
> He intends to Re-open the Shop lately occupied by Mr. M'Quaker in Palmerin-street, and commence Business therein as a
>
> **BAKER & CONFECTIONER.**
>
> R. BURNETT hopes that by supplying his Customers with the best of Bread and Small Goods of the very best description, he will receive a fair share of support.
>
> ☞ Wedding or any other Cakes will be made to order at the shortest notice.
> 687   **ROBERT BURNETT.**

WED 14 SEP 1881. P2. WET

By 1890, he had become the Chairman of the Stanthorpe Divisional Board,[27] and continued to serve for the next decade, being elected chairman for the ninth time in 1904,[28] after the Division became a Shire.[g]

---

f The photograph on p. 79 was taken after 1881 when the business was owned by H. Teitzel and shows clearly that the building housed two different businesses.

g The *Divisional Boards Act 1879* established a new form of local government by dividing all unincorporated parts of Queensland into 74 divisions, and creating for each an elected divisional board which was responsible for a range of services and amenities within its area. Each board had a number of councillors, and a chairman who was appointed from amongst their number. The Stanthorpe Division was created on 11 November 1879. In 1902, the *Local Authorities Act* replaced all divisions with shires. This took effect on 31 March 1903.

> **WARWICK FLOUR.**
>
> TO THE EDITOR OF THE WARWICK ARGUS.
>
> SIR,—I was greatly astonished to read a debate in the Assembly last week in which it was stated that the Warwick flour would not keep. Now I have been connected with the baking business since I was 12 years of age, and during that long experience up to the present date I have not used better flour than I have obtained from the two mills in Warwick during the past twelve months. The last six months the flour seemed to improve in strength and quality, showing consequently that age improved it, and if such is the case, as developement will illustrate, we shall certainly have no need to go outside our own colony for our daily bread and other produce.
> —Yours truly,
>
> W. H. McQUAKER.
>
> Stanthorpe, October 12.

SAT 17 OCT 1891. P2. WA

But the McQuaker story did not end there.

He and Fanny had five children, including their first son who, confusingly, shared his father's name. However, he was to become a widower for the second time when Fanny died on 15 January 1888, leaving him to care for his young family, including a toddler.

Two years later, on 25 January 1900, he married Martha Coleman, and their son, West Hamilton Coleman McQuaker, was born on 10 October 1900. Less than a fortnight later, on 22 October 1900, Martha, too, died, possibly due to complications following the birth. The baby was adopted by one of Martha's sisters and became part of the well-known McQuaker family in the Barcaldine district.

West Hamilton McQuaker himself died in Stanthorpe on 1 May 1913, but his two sons (West Hamilton and West Hamilton Coleman) carried on the family name – if not the baking trade.

Joseph and Mrs Stockbridge

The earliest mention found of Joseph Stockbridge and his wife is in 1869 when they made several generous contributions to the St Mark's Building Fund. The first time his wholesale and retail business as a 'confectioner, pastry cook, fancy bread and biscuit maker' is mentioned is on 12 March 1870 in the *Warwick Examiner and Times* when he advertises that he has taken over the Palmerin St premises of a Mrs Millar.

> **Pure Unadulterated Digestive Bread.**
>
> ## J. STOCKBRIDGE,
> **BAKER, CONFECTIONER, ETC.,**
>
> BEGS to inform his customers and friends that he has
>
> ### REMOVED
>
> To those commodious premises lately occupied by Mrs. Millar, in Palmerin-street, and takes the present opportunity of thanking his friends for the liberal support he has received since commencing business, and would solicit the continuance of their favors.
>
> **WEDDING AND CHRISTENING CAKES MADE TO ORDER.** 138

SAT 12 MAR 1870. P3. WET

Later named Warwick Bakery, the business diversified into fruit by May 1873, in response to the 'extortionate prices'[29] being charged by other fruiterers.

> **Fruit !   Fruit !   Fruit !**
>
> **Preliminary Notice.**
>
> ## J. STOCKBRIDGE,
> PALMERIN-STREET,
>
> WILL, on and after the 1st May, have on sale,
>
> ### FIRST-CLASS FRUIT,
>
> Which he has arranged to sell at very much LOWER PRICES than is now paid for Fruit. N B.—Extortionate prices done away with after that date.
>
> J. STOCKBRIDGE,
> 529   Palmerin-street, Warwick.

SAT 3 MAY 1873. P3. WET

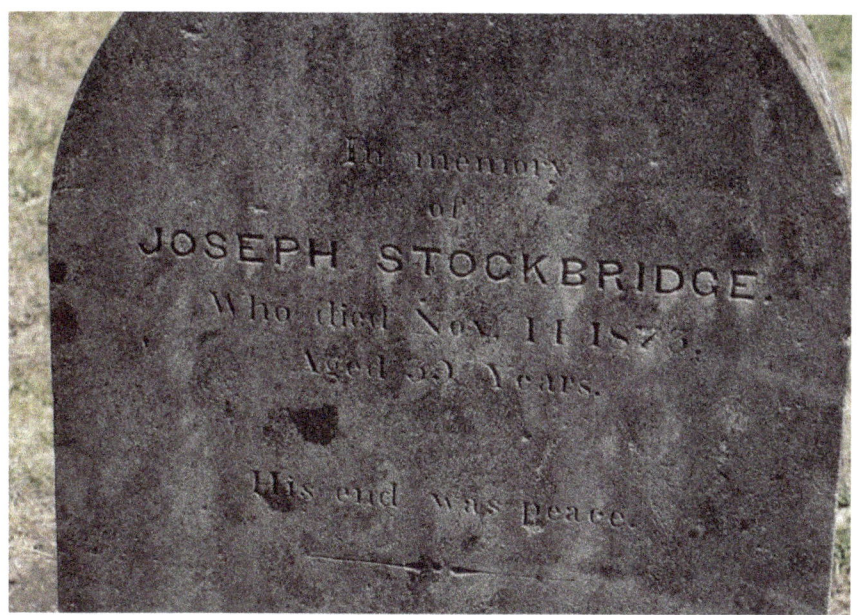

Joseph Stockbridge's gravestone in the old Church of England section of the Warwick Cemetery. The inscription reads '*In memory of Joseph Stockbridge who died 14 November 1873, aged 39 years. His end was peace*'. (Photograph courtesy of Eric Turner.)

When Joseph died unexpectedly on 14 November that year at the age of just 39,[30] Mrs Stockbridge immediately took over the business, engaging a baker and advertising for a boy to operate the baker's cart. By the time of the eighth annual exhibition, held in the Town Hall by the Eastern Downs Horticultural and Agricultural Association in February 1874, she was winning accolades for the whiteness of the bread her bakery had produced from flour milled in Warwick – an 'object of admiration of all who saw it', according to the newspaper report.[31]

SAT 6 DEC 1873. P2. WET

However, by July 1874, Mrs Stockbridge had relinquished the bakery and confectionary business, advertising the sale of the plant and equipment as well as her collection of glassware, china and plateware.[32] Nothing daunted, within a month she was back in business, this time engaging a 'first class milliner and dressmaker' for her new Ladies' Warehouse in premises next to the Bank of New South Wales,[33] while the bakery business was purchased by Mr J.P. Ross, a baker, pastrycook and confectioner.

To Hotelkeepers, Bakers, Dealers, and Private Families.

AUCTION.   AUCTION.

C. B. DAVENEY

HAS received instruction from Mrs. STOCKBRIDGE, who is relinquishing the Bakery Business, to submit to Public Auction, all the

STOCK-IN-TRADE
of
Her Valuable Bakery and Confectionery Business.

The Confectionery consists of every delicacy to be found in the first-class establishment of its kind and in large quantities, but will be lotted to suit the private individuals as well as the business man.

The Gilmont's Stores
Are of the best brands and of every variety.

Cut and Show Glasses.
Of exquisite design consisting of Champagne, Claret, Wine, Jelly, and Custard Glasses, Finger Glasses, Glass Dishes, Decanters—Pints and Quarts.

The China
Consists of 4 Sets of Dessert Services, Cups and Saucers, Milk Jugs, 4 Salad Bowls.

Platedware.
Forks, large and small, Table Spoons, Dessert, and Tea Spoons, Covered Jugs, Knives. Many of these goods are new and in quantities sufficient for an Hotel.

The Bakery
Is wanting in nothing and is replete with every article for a first-class business.
A large 20 gallon Fountain new
An Assortment of Tools
And many other useful Lots.

Sale on the Premises, on THURSDAY and FRIDAY, 23rd and 24th instants.

N.B.—The Confectionary and Shop Goods will be sold the First Day.
Sale will commence at 11 o'clock each day.

SAT 18 JUL 1874. P2. WET

New Ladies' Warehouse
AND
MILLINERY AND DRESSMAKING ESTABLISHMENT.

MRS. STOCKBRIDGE

BEGS to inform the Ladies of Warwick and surrounding districts, that she will

OPEN BUSINESS

As above, on or about TUESDAY, AUGUST 19, In those premises

IN PALMERIN-STREET,

lately occupied by Mr. Greiner, Watchmaker, and next to the Bank of New South Wales.

She will always have in STOCK
A CHOICE SELECTION
OF
Ladies' & Children's Clothing, Boots, &c.

Having secured the services of a
FIRST CLASS MILLINER & DRESSMAKER, she will be prepared to execute all orders in the Neatest Style and Latest Fashion.   706

SAT 15 AUG 1874. P2. WET

J. P. ROSS,
BAKER, PASTRYCOOK, AND CONFECTIONER,

BEGS to announce to the Public of Warwick and vicinity, that he has OPENED that

BAKERY ESTABLISHMENT

Lately carried on by MRS. STOCKBRIDGE, where he intends to carry on BAKING and PASTRYCOOKING in all its branches, and hopes that by strict attention, sobriety, and the lowest possible profits, to merit a fair share of public patronage.

Bread of the best quality and everything of the best material.

Prize Medal, London Exhibition, 1862, for Ornamental Bride, Christening, and Birthday Cakes.

All orders turned out with despatch.

HOT PIES every SATURDAY EVENING, from 4 till 11 o'clock. 710

SAT 3 OCT 1874. P1. WET

New Goods suitable for the Present Season.

MRS. STOCKBRIDGE

WOULD remind her friends and the public that the ENLARGEMENTS TO HER PREMISES Are now completed, and that she has just Received, and is now Showing, a Choice and Well-assorted Stock of

New and Fashionable Goods,

INCLUDING—
Hats, Bonnets, Trimmings, Ribbons, Dress Pieces, Dresses (Ready-made), Skirts, Underclothing, Boys' Suits, Boots and Shoes, &c., &c.;
also a Choice Assortment of

Fancy Goods and Toys.

Dresses made up on the Premises in the Latest Style.

☞ Note the address — Palmerin-street, next to the Bank of New South Wales.

SAT 19 DEC 1874. P3. WET

SATURDAY, MAY 9.

Auction Sale of HOUSEHOLD FURNITURE, Sewing Machines, and Kitchen Effects.

C. B. DAVENEY is instructed by Mrs. Stockbridge (who is leaving by the May steamer for London) to sell, at her residence, corner of Guy and Fitzroy streets, on SATURDAY, May 9, at 11 o'clock—

All her FURNITURE and EFFECTS, without the Slightest Reserve; they consist of—

Large Oval Table, Glassware, Books, Pictures, Chairs, small Cedar Table, 2 Easy Chairs, Hearth Rug, Chiffonier, Matting, Antimacassars, Couch, 2 Ottomans, 8 day Clock, Lamp, Vases, Ornaments, Table Cover, Lace Curtains, Blinds and Vallances, double Iron Bedstead, Washstand and Ware, Quilts, Chest Drawers, Window Blinds, Dressing Table, Looking Glass, Sheets, Palliass, Mattrass, Matting, Mosquito Net

WORK ROOM—Table, 4 Cedar Chairs, Lamp, Blinds, 4 Sewing Machines.

KITCHEN—Table, Pine Safe, Boiler, Sauce Pans, Fry Pan, Kettle, Washing Tubs, Crockery Ware, China Cups and Saucers, Pot Plants, Door Mats, and numerous other articles.

SAT 2 MAY 1885. P3. WA

By September 1874,[34] Mr Ross had begun proudly advertising his London credentials (and the fact that he would be selling hot pies every Saturday evening) while Mrs Stockbridge continued to develop her millinery and dressmaking business, expanding her premises and range of goods by Christmas that year.

The last mention found of Mrs Stockbridge is in 1885[35] when she sold up and returned to the UK.

INTO THE TWENTIETH CENTURY

From the late nineteenth century, as Warwick's population and prosperity grew, bakeries multiplied. Many of these businesses were short-lived; others served the community and the district for many years. The larger bakery businesses of this era are described in alphabetical order below; many others are acknowledged under Warwick's Bakehouses (p. 137) and Our Daily Bread (p. 167).

Richard Emil Bochman

Richard Emil Bochman was born in Oberlungwitz in the German state of Sachsen (Saxony) in 1889. His mother died when he was very young but, raised by his father and stepmother, he became an apprentice baker, receiving his trade certificate 'for his efforts, achievements and general good behaviour' from the bakers' guild in Dresden on 11 May 1906, the day after his 17th birthday.

Bochman then joined the Imperial German navy and among the vessels on which he served was the *Roon*, an armoured cruiser which plied the route from

Germany to the north-eastern part of the island of New Guinea when it was a German protectorate.[h]

It was during one such voyage that Bochman first visited Australia.

The crew list for that voyage (p. 44) records that Emil Bochmann (one of several spellings of his name) was a 19-year-old 'pantry-washman'. He took shore leave in Sydney when the ship docked on 16 December 1908 and the photograph below shows that Christmas (Weihnachten) was celebrated while the *Roon* was in port in Sydney.

Richard Bochman is seated, far right. His friend, Hermann ('Alf') Moses, is standing behind him with his hands on Richard's shoulders. (Photographs courtesy of Neil Roderick.)

h   Known as Kaiser-Wilhelmsland from 1884 until the outbreak of WWI in 1914 when the territory fell to Australian forces.

[Ship manifest image showing handwritten passenger and crew list with header "INWARD. A LIST of the Crew and Passengers arrived in the Ship Roon of Br— of the Burthen of 5133 Nett/Gross Tons, from the Port of Bremerhaven to Sydney, Norddeutscher Lloyd—Lohmann & Co."]

Bochman continued to serve in the German navy, next appearing in photographs as a member of the crew of the *SMS*[i] *Thüringen*, one of the great battleships of the Imperial German fleet. As the *Thüringen* was not commissioned until June 1911, the humorous photograph of him on page 45 probably dates from c. 1912. Bochman is on the far right, smoking one of the trademark cigars which he continued to enjoy throughout his long life,[j] and he is pointing to his friend's empty wallet – a reference to the message written on the barrel: 'Wieder Sonntag ohne Geld' (Another Sunday without money).

At some point before WWI, Bochman returned to Australia. He first found work as a baker in Redfern in Sydney, but anti-German sentiment in Australia at that time meant that he was not made to feel welcome.

His response was to leave Redfern to work on the railways, eventually finding work as a baker in a hotel in the Riverina town of Temora, north of Wagga Wagga. This would have been much more congenial for him because, from the 1860s, the southern Riverina had been settled by Germans relocating from South Australia and Victoria.

On 22 September 1917, he married Letitia Corcoran, the cook at the hotel where he worked. They established a family home at Gardner St, Temora, while Richard worked as a baker in the town. Their son Austin Anthony was born a year later and on 31 January 1922, Bochman was granted a Certificate of Naturalisation.[36] Their daughter Clare (named after County Clare in her mother's native Ireland) was born in Temora in October 1922.

At some point between Clare's birth and 1925, the family moved to

---

i   Abbreviation for Seiner Majestäts Schiff (His Majesty's Ship) as used by the German Navy (Kaiserliche Marine).
j   On his death, a large number of cigar boxes was found in his flat in Warwick and his grandson, Neil Roderick, still uses them to store photographs.

Warwick. West's Bakery in Grafton St was acquired in February 1925, and the first advertisement for Bochman's Central Bakery appeared in the *Catholic Advocate* on 16 April 1925. Bochman was clearly very enterprising and successful because, by 1931, he had acquired the adjacent block of land to construct a block of shops and flats, the Bochman Buildings.

ESTATE late Dr. Hunt, premises occupied as Vulcanising Works, adjoining West's bakery, Grafton street, can be altered for shop and residence. Low price and easy terms. Apply McDOUGALL & CO. 571

SAT 26 JUL 1924. P6.

CENTRAL BAKERY,
Grafton Street :: Warwick.
R. Bochman
Baker and Pastrycook, Wedding and Birthday Cakes a Speciality. Functions supplied. Rail and motor delivery service daily. 'Phone. 417.

THURS 16 APR 1925. P35. CATHOLIC ADVOCATE

(Photograph courtesy of Neil Roderick.)

Bochman's Bakery c. 1926 with the Bochman children, Austin and Clare, in the delivery vehicle. (Photograph courtesy of Neil Roderick.)

Hermann Alfred Moses. (Photograph courtesy of Peter McKenzie.)

In 1932, he leased his bakery to Lloyd and Henry ('Harry') Crone (p. 67) for seven years and undertook a six-month visit to his native Germany. On his return, *The Brisbane Courier* carried a detailed report (below) on 21 April 1933. It should be noted that Adolf Hitler did not attain power until March that year, just before Bochman's return to Warwick.

GERMANY TO-DAY
A Visitor's Impressions

Mr R. Bochman, who has returned to Warwick from a tour embracing Germany, Belgium, and Holland, states that although he had travelled extensively through Germany he saw nothing verging on a state of persecution of Jewish business people.

He attended election meetings in Germany, and listened to speeches by Herr Hitler, who did not display the slightest antagonism towards Jewish business people, although he had given what was tantamount to a pledge that if his party and the Stahlhelms[k] were placed in power one of the first actions would be the displacement of Jews from high Government offices. These posts would now revert to Germans, although Jews would still be employed in minor positions.

While in Germany Mr Bochman said he was surprised to read in the English newspapers of the alleged persecution of Jews. A majority of large stores and many chain stores throughout the country were controlled by Jews, and it was astonishing how cheaply the articles were sold by them.

There were no signs of extreme distress or poverty in Germany today, and places of amusement were always well patronised. Wireless was very popular. Wages were low in comparison with Australia, averaging about £2 a week for the ordinary working man and 15/- for factory girls. Those who were unemployed received 13/- a week from the Government during the period they were out of work. As soon as they found employment, however, it was obligatory to repay the Government part of that money in instalments of a few shillings a week.

---

k   Literally 'steel helmets', a reference to German military uniforms of the time.

On his return from Germany, Bochman launched ambitious plans to extend his eponymous buildings. The 1934 extension enabled the number of flats to be increased and created a space for a dental surgery which he hoped would one day be occupied by his son, Austin. As Austin matriculated only in February 1935, this was somewhat premature, but he did go on to study Dentistry at Sydney University and to a long and successful career as a dentist in Sydney.

In 1937, Bochman's old friend from the German navy, Hermann Alfred ('Alf') Moses (p. 46), became the licensee of the Australian Hotel in Warwick and continued to operate it with his wife Sarah (née Douglas) until the 1940s.

The smartly redecorated Bochman's Bakery building c. 1931 with the first stage of the adjacent Bochman Buildings. The Dainty Café (Bochman's Café from February 1932) and the Warwick Fruit Mart were early tenants of the shops. Others included a costumier/milliner and a fish monger. (Photograph courtesy of David Glasgow, source and photographer unidentified.)

After the death of his wife Letitia in October 1963, Bochman continued to live in their flat at 72A Fitzroy St until his death in 1981 at the age of 93. Both are buried in the Warwick cemetery.

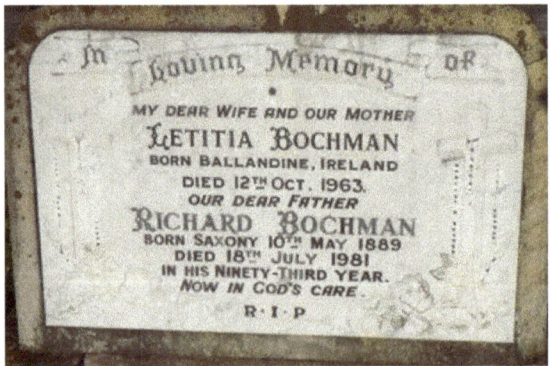

The headstone on the grave of Richard and Letitia Bochman in Warwick Cemetery was erected by their children, Austin and Clare. (Photograph courtesy of Eric Turner.)

The Bochman Buildings in 2020, showing the 1934 extension to the left of the original building. (Author's photograph, September 2020.)

The Bochman Buildings were inherited by their children, Austin and Clare, and remained in the Bochman family until 2009 when they were sold to Peta McKenzie, and Leanne Munson. Their respective husbands, Paul Munson and Peter McKenzie (the grandson of 'Alf' Moses) were business partners in Darling Downs Insurance Brokers. In 2020, ownership remained unchanged and Darling Downs Insurance Brokers were still a tenant of the building.

Although Richard Bochman lived in Warwick until his death in 1981 at the age of 93, his attachment to Germany remained strong. A memory of his homeland (the imposing Burg Kriebstein, towering above the Zschopau River near Erlau in Saxony) was painted directly onto a wall in his flat in the Bochman Buildings. Both Richard and his son Austin were talented artists but it is not known whether this was their work. (Author's photograph, September 2020.)

Burg Kriebstein (Kriebstein Castle) close to Bochman's birthplace.[37]

Martin and Ralph Brown

Martin Brown purchased the bakery at 41 Albion St in October 1933 and ran Brown's Bakery until his retirement in 1951. His son, Ralph, purchased the business from him and expanded it by opening a shop in the Club Hotel building in Palmerin St in 1954. He operated the business with his wife Amy until her death in February 1963. Ralph sold the business to Joe and Mary Hall in 1966; Martin returned to his native USA in 1967; and Ralph left Warwick in 1971.

Brown's Bakery at the southern end of the Club Hotel building.
(*Warwick Daily News*, photographer and date unidentified.)

Martin Brown

Martin Ralph Brown was born into a family of Swedish immigrant farmers in 1889 in Rockford, Illinois, USA. Just before his third birthday, his mother contracted typhoid fever and died, leaving Martin and his brother Robert to be cared for by his father. Six years later, his father remarried and moved his family to El Campo in Texas. However, Martin did not get on well with his stepmother and, from the age of 14, regularly left home, working his way from job to job on farms in Texas as well as on the Southern Pacific Railroad in Oakland, California. He eventually reached Vancouver where he found work as a cook for a bridge-building gang in a logging camp. The photograph below shows Martin, far left, at the age of 20 in his cook's apron.

(Photograph from author's collection.)

Some years after the 1906 San Francisco earthquake, Martin and a friend visited the city, curious to see the destruction caused by the quake. San Francisco at the time was a lawless town and, not surprisingly, they were robbed. With nothing to lose, they tossed their only remaining coin to decide whether to go to the Klondike and pan for gold, or to New Zealand. When the toss favoured New Zealand, Martin worked his passage there, arriving in Wellington in March 1912 and finding work on construction of the railway to connect the isolated East Coast of the North Island with Rotorua and Auckland

In New Zealand, Martin met Edith Ball, a nurse from Rangiora, near Christchurch in the South Island. They married there on 30 September 1914 and went to live in the remote North Island settlement of Motuhora. The next year, their first child, Dorothy Selma, was born in Gisborne (the closest hospital); their second child, Ralph Ashley, was born in Rangiora, three and a half years later.

At some point, Martin had contracted tuberculosis. Advised by a doctor to move to a warmer climate, he lived in Fiji for a year while his wife and two children stayed with her family in Rangiora.

(Photograph from author's collection.)

On his return, Martin moved the family back to the North Island where he worked in a sawmill at Raetihi, in the shadow of Mt Ruapehu, eventually setting up a mill of his own in the nearby village of Mataroa.

(Photograph from author's collection.)

Martin Brown (centre) with mill workers in Raetihi, New Zealand, in the early 1930s. (Photograph from author's collection.)

However, the impact of the Great Depression on the timber industry was severe and this prompted him to consider moving his family to Australia.

Although his experience of baking was limited to working in the lumber camp in British Columbia, he had made enquiries about buying a bakery in Australia and, on arrival in Brisbane in April 1933, decided to proceed with the purchase of the bakery at 41 Albion St, Warwick. His son, Ralph, had just turned 14 when they immigrated and immediately began work in the bakery alongside his father.

The business did not prosper initially – within a year, Martin had taken the previous owner, Percy St Henry, to court (and won) for misrepresenting the volume of sales. He even contemplated selling the business as early as March 1936, but the would-be purchaser, H.A. Conley, was 'unable to complete the sale' for 'private reasons'.[38] However, by end of the decade, the business began to do well and Martin started to take a leading role in the trade in Warwick.

He developed improved delivery carts; became the President of the Warwick Bread Manufacturers Association and the Warwick Bread Distributing Company; and won the championship for his bread in Warwick's Centenary Show in 1940. He also became a member of the Rotary Club of Warwick and donated an American flag to the Warwick City Council to fly on 4 July, America's national day.

(Photograph from author's collection.)

Martin's activity was not confined to baking. As a self-taught carpenter and mechanic, he built several boats in NZ and Australia and a total of three caravans in Warwick. After he retired in 1951, Martin and Edith (always accompanied by the family dog) fished their way up and down the Queensland coast every winter until Edith's death in 1957.

He retained his US citizenship throughout his time in NZ and Australia and, in 1967, returned to the USA permanently. Driven by curiosity and a desire for knowledge, he remained an adventurer and inveterate traveller – and a highly successful fisherman – to the end of his life. He died in Conroe, Texas, in November 1979, just a week before his 90th birthday.

The Brown family (L-R) Ralph, Amy, Edith and Judith Brown with Martin Brown in the cab of the Blitz truck used to haul *Far Horizons*, the first of three caravans he built in Warwick. (Photograph from author's collection, 1949.)

Martin Brown at Lucinda Point, North Queensland, in the 1950s and in Belize, Central America, in 1974. (Photographs from author's collection.)

Ralph Brown

Ralph Ashley Brown was born in Rangiora, near Christchurch in New Zealand's South Island, in April 1919.

He grew up and went to school in Raetihi and Mataroa, small timber towns in the centre of the North Island, and came to Australia with his parents and older sister in 1933, just before his 14th birthday.

He worked for his father, Martin, for the next seven years both in the bakery at 41 Albion St and as a carter, delivering bread around town and to farms and settlements in the district.

On 30 December 1940, aged 21, he was sworn in to the RAAF in Brisbane. After basic training at the Richmond air base in NSW and

Ralph aged c. 12 with eel at Mataroa, NZ.
(Photograph from author's collection.)

the Melbourne Technical College, he was posted to the No.1 Engineering School at Ascot Vale in Melbourne. After a short posting in Maryborough, Queensland, as a Leading Aircraftsman, he was transferred to the Amberley air base to assemble US aircraft – Kitty Hawk, Aircobra and Vultee Vengeance.

He married Amy Radford on 24 April 1943 and immediately afterwards was posted to Melbourne for a 12-week Junior NCOs course. He then returned to Amberley where he served until April 1945 when he was posted to Townsville. He remained there until his discharge on 26 November 1945.

Before joining the Air Force, Ralph had developed skills as a carpenter and mechanic, working alongside his father. His five years' service added training and experience as a fitter and turner. This useful combination was put to use building a family home on the block of land beside the bakery in Albion St as well as inventing and building various machines and other equipment for use in the bakery, including a machine to make breadcrumbs from left-over bread.

Ralph continued to work for his father until Martin retired. He then bought the business in 1951 and opened a successful bakery shop in the Club Hotel building in Palmerin St in 1954, expanding the range of products to include cakes, pastries, sliced bread, and the bakery's famed cream buns.

He served for a term as an Alderman on Warwick City Council and became an active, long-standing member of the Rotary Club in Warwick and, in retirement, on the Sunshine Coast. He lived in Buderim, Queensland, with his second wife, Valerie, his two sons (Calvin and Peter) and adopted children (Evan and Lindy) until his death in 1999 at the age of 80. In accordance with his wishes, his ashes were scattered in the waters of the Hautapu River which flows through the haunts of his boyhood in Mataroa.

Ralph Brown (centre), Luna Park, Melbourne, 11 February 1941.
(Photograph from author's collection.)

Ralph in his 'Brown's Special', the three-wheeled car he built, modelled on the Morgan and powered by an Indian motorbike engine. (Photograph from author's collection.)

Breadcrumb grinding machine designed and built by Ralph. (Photograph from author's collection.)

BREAD
(Judge: Mr McKenna, Stanthorpe)
Two loaves of bread (open to master bakers and employees in the Warwick city area): Clark and Glasby 1. R. A. Brown 2.
Two loaves of bakers' bread (open to master bakers and employees outside Warwick city area): N. R. Anderson.
Wholemeal bread (open) any shape: R. A. Brown 1. M. R. Brown 2.
Champion loaf of bread: R. A. Brown.

THU 13 FEB 1947, P6.

Ralph repeated his father's 1940 success when he won the Champion Loaf of Bread in the 1947 Warwick Show.

The house at 39 Albion St beside Brown's Bakery. Built by Ralph in 1946-1947 while his family lived in an Army tent in the back yard, he named it 'Ralamy' – a combination of his and his wife's first names. The house remained the Brown family home until 1966 when the bakery was sold to Joe and Mary Hall. It then became home to another baking family, Owen and Margaret Mollenhauer of Mollies Cake Shop. (Photograph from author's collection.)

Ralph Brown on the 1925 Harley Davidson which came to Australia with the Brown family from NZ in 1933. Fitted with a sidecar, it became the principal means of transport for Ralph, Amy, their daughter Judith and their faithful dog, Gyp, for several years after WWII. (Photograph from author's collection.)

Stanley Cain and Alfred Thorne

Alec Stanley Munro ('Stan') Cain was born in Warwick in August 1913 and first entered the baking trade as an apprentice pastrycook and cake decorator, indentured to German baker, Richard Bochman, at 76 Grafton St (p. 42).

By October 1932, aged just 19, Stan had established a business partnership with his friend, Alfred Thorne, advertising the opening of the Cain and Thorne bakery on the corner of Percy St and Oak Avenue, next to the Cain family home at 61 Percy St[39] (p. 161).

As this was the height of the Great Depression, it was not an easy time to establish a business, and the new partners faced stiff competition from others in the trade. For example, the source of bakers' flour was highly contentious at this time because flour purchased from interstate was cheaper, enabling bakers to reduce their costs, increase their profits, and gain a competitive advantage. In 1933, Cain and Thorne tendered for the valuable contract to supply the Warwick Hospital, offering a price of just 2½ d. per loaf compared with 4 d. a loaf offered by the only other tenderer. Many column inches of newspaper space were dedicated to a verbatim report of the heated discussion at a meeting of the hospital Board as to whether the Cain and Thorne tender should be accepted if there was no proof that they had used only Queensland flour.[40]

The pressure of competition may also have been behind rumours that circulated the following year that Cain and Thorne were selling their business. Whether or not this was the reason, Cain and Thorne found it necessary to insert an 'Important Notice' in the paper in November 1934, emphatically denying the rumours.[41]

Competition continued into 1936 when an unnamed baker went to the extent of lodging an anonymous complaint with the Industrial Inspector in Brisbane that three of his competitors in Warwick (Cain and Thorne, V. Elsley and Sons and Tucker Brothers) were all in breach of the prescribed starting time for bakers.[42]

Cain and Thorne's business nevertheless flourished. Regular advertisements appeared throughout 1936 for their delivery service, their milk and wholemeal bread, and their 'fine textured and beautifully flavoured loaf',[43] and they adopted the name The Royal Bakery.[44]

In 1937, despite yet another fine for an award breach,[45] Stan's personal situation improved. First, ownership of the land and bakery was transferred

Stanley and Valma Cain. (Photograph courtesy of Janice Aldred.)

to him and his older brother, George, by their mother, Mary.[46] Then, on 26 August 1937, he married Valma ('Val') McFarlane, the sister of another Warwick baker, William Neville ('Nev') McFarlane, who worked at Ward's bakery. Stan's business partner, Alf Thorne, was Best Man at the wedding.

An advertisement in early 1940 for 'two reliable cart geldings, 4 to 5 years',[47] and an advertorial for The Royal Bakery the following year[48] were the last occasions on which the business is mentioned in the Warwick newspaper. While Electoral Rolls for 1943 show Stan and Val still registered at 'Valstyn' in Lyons St, according to family records, they sold the Percy St bakery in 1942 and established a new business in Clifton, c. 50 km from Toowoomba.

That business proved to be very successful and was sold in May 1945, enabling Stan and Val to take a six-week holiday on the Gold Coast. They lived in Toowoomba for the remainder of that year, awaiting the birth of their daughter, Janice, but returned to the Gold Coast early in 1946 to establish a new bakery – transporting the six-week-old Janice in a laundry basket.

While the bakery in the main street of Surfers Paradise was successful, the family was on the move again by the end of that year, prompted in part by Val's asthma, but made more urgent by the development of the dreaded 'rope' bacillus in the wooden troughs and benches at the bakery (p. 107).

Undeterred, the entrepreneurial Stan quickly established Valstyn Cake Shop in 1947 in Beaudesert Rd in the Brisbane suburb of Moorooka, with the family living in nearby Mackie St. By 1948, he had opened a second establishment in a block of three shops which he built in Fegen Dr, Moorooka. In the 1950s, he diversified, first opening a combined snack bar and cake shop in Ipswich Rd, Moorooka, and then establishing his 'Caketeria' further along Ipswich Rd in the suburb of Annerley in 1954. Surrounded by industry, the 'Caketeria' thrived, but Stan had still more plans, opening his fifth and final Brisbane cake shop, 'Janval' (named for his wife Valma and daughter Janice), in 1962 on the opposite side of Ipswich Rd in Annerley.

Five years later, Stan suffered a heart attack and, while it was not fatal, he did scale down his activities, working in the cake section of Woolworths and as a relief pastrycook in other businesses until he retired at the age of 67, after half a century in the trade. When the business was sold in 1980, he and Val made their final move – to 'Little Valstyn' in McCullough St, Sunnybank.

Such was Stan's interest in his chosen trade that he became the sole male member of the Queensland Cake Decorators' Association, and the Central Branch of the Association awarded him Honorary Membership for his outstanding contribution to the craft. He was to have received the award at the Association's Christmas party in 1989, but died on 20 November that year. The award was proudly accepted in his stead by his wife Val and daughter Janice.

Stan Cain at the wheel of his proudly branded delivery van in Clifton.
(Photograph courtesy of Janice Aldred.)

Stan and Val Cain established their first home in Lyons St, Warwick, combining their given names to call it 'Valstyn'. (Photograph courtesy of Janice Aldred.)

Details of Alfred Thorne's life have been more difficult to establish. It is known that he and Stan Cain were firm friends and that his role in the bakery business was principally as a delivery driver and general roustabout. Nevertheless, there is one specific mention of him as a baker in the Electoral Roll of 1943 when he and his wife, Ethel Helena Jessie, were living in Wantley St, Warwick. Alf and Ethel next appeared in the 1954 Roll by which stage they had moved to 18 Newman St (now Road) in Moorooka – just blocks away from their friends Stan and Val Cain in Mackie St. The Thornes remained in Newman St for more than 20 years until they retired to Scarborough. Despite the move, their friendship with the Cains continued, with Alf and Ethel attending the Cains' fortieth wedding anniversary celebration in 1987.

Clarke and Glasby

Harold Gordon ('Gordon') Clarke was a baker in Murwillumbah, Northern New South Wales, before purchasing Otto Meyer's bakery business at 58 Grafton St, Warwick, in July 1939. He continued Meyer's deliveries and his range of bakery lines, including 'Glyx' bread ('the body builder',[49] made from soy flour) and 'Cerevite', a product described by Queensland Cereal Industries Pty Ltd as 'stabilised wheat-germ bread' with 'a minimum content of 10 per cent wheat germ' in compliance with the State Health Department's regulations governing 'bread stuff'.[50]

UNDER NEW MANAGEMENT
MEYER'S BAKERY
This Business has been purchased by H. G. CLARKE, late of Murwillumbah, who assures the Public of Warwick of his Best Services at all times. Become a regular client To-day. Order your White, Brown, Wholemeal, Malt, Cerevite and Glyx Bread, Buns, and Bun Loaves from the new baker—
H. G. CLARKE, Grafton-street, Warwick. Phone 564

TUE 18 JUL 1939. P5.

Clarke later formed a business partnership, trading as Clarke and Glasby, and by the mid-1940s had become one of the six major bread manufacturers in the city alongside Brown's, Crone's, Parker's, Tucker's and the Warwick Bakery. Advertising and other records indicate that the business continued to trade successfully until at least the mid-1950s.

As this newspaper report demonstrates, like other bakeries, Clarke and Glasby operated under the watchful eye of Industrial

Breach of Award
—o—
Baker Fined

Harold Gordon Clark, of the firm of Clark and Glasby, pleaded guilty in the Industrial Magistrate's Court yesterday before Mr. H. B. Carney, S.M., to a charge that he committed a breach of the Bakers and Pastrycooks' Award (Southern and Mackay District) in that he allowed an employee, Patrick Slattery, to do baker's work before the prescribed time of 5 a.m.

TUE 18 MAR 1947. P2.

65

Inspectors who were constantly on the lookout for award breaches, particularly cases of starting to bake earlier than the prescribed time of 5.00 am.

Clarke died on 17 July 1959, at the age of 52 and was buried in the Warwick cemetery.

No definitive information has been found about Glasby. There may be a connection to H.G. Glasby who briefly owned Elseys bakery in Palmerin St, but no link has yet been established.

'Gordon' Clarke's headstone in the Warwick cemetery. (Photograph courtesy of Eric Turner.)

Lloyd and Henry ('Harry') Crone

Brothers Lloyd James Herbert and John Henry Hill ('Harry') Crone were bakers in Brisbane before leasing Richard Bochman's bakery at 76 Grafton St, Warwick, on 21 October 1932.

They had inspected the oven beforehand and knew that the furnace and crown needed repair but nevertheless signed a six-year lease, with an option of renewal for a further four, believing that repairs were the responsibility of the owner. When Bochman claimed he was not responsible, the Department of Public Health was called in to conduct an inspection. The Department ordered repairs in February 1935 but, as Bochman still claimed he was not responsible, it was left to the Crones to carry out the repairs themselves. They then attempted to claim the expense through the courts but, almost three years after signing the lease, the case was finally resolved in favour of Bochman in August that year.

The Crones, like most Warwick bakeries, always did a roaring trade at Christmas baking hams. Families brought their whole hams to the bakery to be wrapped in dough and baked. The smell of baking ham and the taste of the fat-soaked bread remains a memory for most bakery staff and their families.

SAVE WORRY !
Let us **BAKE YOUR XMAS HAM.**
PRICE 7/6.
All hams must be in by 5.30 Friday.
CRONE'S BAKERY
76 Grafton Street, Warwick.

THU 20 DEC 1951. P2.

In the early 1950s, the CSIRO and the Bread Research Institute developed a method of incorporating milk into bread using powdered milk. At the same time, this solved a dairy surplus and the public responded well to the product. The Crones were among the early adopters in Warwick, although Cain and Thorne, as early as 1936, were advertising that 'the addition of Nestle's Milk ensures a better cutting loaf'.[51]

The Crones operated the business together until 1950 when Lloyd and his wife, Alice Georgina (née Mewes) moved to Redcliffe, selling his interest in the business to Harry. Only three years later, on 30 June 1953, Lloyd died in Brisbane, aged 45 – another in the series of Warwick bakers who died well before their time. His death was reported in the *Warwick Daily News* the following day. (See below right.)

Harry continued to run the business until the late 1950s after which the bakery building was sold to the Country Women's Association (p. 158). Harry appeared in Electoral Rolls as a Master Baker in Warwick until 1963, after which he and his wife, Henrietta Jessie (née Lamb), moved to the Brisbane suburb of Sherwood where he worked as a storeman. Four years after his wife's death in 1976, the Electoral Roll records him living at the Freemasons' Home in Sandgate where he died on 27 February 1983.

Research on Milk Loaf Successful

MELBOURNE: Milk bread of high quality can now be made available to the Australian public. Bread made with milk instead of water keeps longer and has better nutritive value. The quality and quantity of protein and the calcium and vitamin B2 contents are increased.

Technical difficulties in the addition of milk solids to bread of the Australian type have been overcome as a result of investigations by the C.S.I.R.O., in conjunction with the Bread Research Institute. A new type of dried milk may be incorporated in bread to the extent of 6 per cent or more to give a milk loaf.

TUE 3 MAR 1953. P3.

The death occurred in the Brisbane General Hospital yesterday of Mr. Lloyd Crone (45), a former Warwick business man. Mr. Crone and his brother conducted the bakery business of Crone Bros. in Grafton Street until about three years ago. Mr. H. Crone then purchased his brother's interest in the business and since then Mr. L. Crone and family have been living at Redcliffe.

WED 1 JUL 1953. P2.

Lloyd Crone with his delivery van. (Date and photographer unknown. Photograph courtesy of Mavis March.)

Memories of Crone's Bakery

'In the early post war years, Crones used to make biscuits as well as bread. I recall the delicious ginger biscuits that they made. All you needed was strong teeth.'

Ted Siebuhr

'Dried fruit in the early 1960s came in large boxes, lined with waxed paper, and had to be washed and dried in the sun before use. Instead of tipping out the water in which the fruit had been washed, Harry used to keep it in a tin in the bakehouse, drinking from it and topping it up as required. Not surprisingly, fermentation occurred, producing a unique baker's tipple.'

Michael Carter

'Harry Crone was early in the battle to produce sliced bread and wrap it in wax paper. This caused much chaos as the shop had to be used for the slicing, and because the hot loaves from the ovens would clog up the slicer, they had to use fans to cool the bread down.'

Ted Siebuhr

Daniel Maunsell

Another of the Irish bakers who found their way to Warwick was Daniel Maunsell.

Born in Limerick in 1858, he came to Australia as a young man and, in common with several others who arrived in Warwick around that time, found work in the Guy St bakery and grocery store of fellow Irish immigrant, John Healy.[52]

Maunsell worked as Healy's master baker for seven years until November 1886 when he was engaged for 12 months as master baker by yet another Irishman, William Brennan, in his 'Warwick Bakery'. This relationship ended unhappily when Brennan sold the bakery to Michael Quigley in March 1877. As Brennan had not informed Maunsell of the sale and the new owner had engaged George Grant as a baker in Maunsell's stead, Maunsell sued Brennan in the Warwick Police Court for '£7, being a week's wages due to him and a week in lieu of notice'.[53]

Maunsell's first premises in Palmerin St were on the eastern side of the street. (Photograph courtesy of David Owens.)

In 1918, Maunsell relocated to John Cantwell's building on the western side of Palmerin St, just south of the Union Bank of Australia (ANZ Bank) building.
(Photograph courtesy of David Owens.)

During the hearing, Maunsell had expressed concern that he would not be able to get further work as a master baker in Warwick and, while the case was decided in his favour, these concerns may have been behind his decision to set up a bakery in Tenterfield, just across the border in New South Wales.

It is not known how long he operated in Tenterfield but by 1898, he had returned to Warwick.[54] He first operated a bakery in Albion St before establishing a bakery and café on the eastern side of Palmerin St, offering hot midday meals and morning and afternoon teas as well as his baked goods. He continued to operate from that site until it was purchased by the then Queensland Government Savings Bank.

The bank's acquisition of the site offered Maunsell the opportunity to relocate to the 'premises for so many years occupied by the late Mr John Cantwell'[1] – another Irishman – on the opposite side of the street. There, he installed a new brick oven and opened The Warwick National Bakery and Refreshment Rooms in March 1918, offering 'first class bread; wedding, christening and all kinds of cakes (large or small)'.[55]

Six months later, his previous bakehouse, shop and other buildings on the eastern side of Palmerin St were demolished, the agent, Mr de Conlay, reporting 'a very successful clearing sale'[56] of scrap iron and building material.

Maunsell continued to operate from his new location with apparent success for the next decade, even entering 'about half a dozen loaves and some assorted buns' in the annual three-day Bread Exhibition in Australia Hall in Sydney in 1926.[57]

---

1   Cantwell died on 16 September 1914 at the age of 78.

Less than two years later, on 28 July 1928, Dan Maunsell died, described in the obituary published in the *Warwick Daily News* as a quiet, unassuming, and generous man who was 'well liked by those who had dealings with him'.[58] The obituary also recognised that, as a tradesman, he was 'said to have had few equals'.

Within a month, Maunsell's widow, Esther Mary Maunsell, had sold the business to L.E. Overstead[59] and by September, had conducted a clearing sale of furniture and effects.[60] The Maunsells had no children, but Mrs Maunsell continued to live in Warwick with her sister Priscilla Kate Tyrell until her death on 9 July 1941, leaving the Maunsell property to Priscilla.[61]

It appears that Cantwell's home, shop and bakery, as well as the premises of Denham Bros. and several other businesses in the section of Palmerin St between the ANZ Bank building (135) and Derby House (149) were demolished because, in 2021, most buildings in this section are built in a style typical of the 1930s. In addition, the building at 141 Palmerin St is known to date from that time. In 2021, no evidence of Cantwell's store or Maunsell's bakery remains.

The approximate location of Maunsell's bakery in Palmerin St in 2021.
(Author's photograph, February 2021.)

Louis, Les and Gordon Overstead

Louis Ellingson Overstead entered the baking trade as a boy in his home town of Stavanger in the south of Norway, arriving in Australia in May 1886 at the age of 20.

On arrival in Warwick, he was employed as a baker by John Healy (p. 24), soon becoming his foreman baker. Within nine years, he was able to set up his own business in Albion St opposite the then Post and Telegraph Office (see advertisement below left). However, from an advertisement in July 1899 (below right), it appears that he returned to work for Healy after four years.

L. E. OVERSTEAD,
Baker and Confectioner
(The last 8 years foreman Baker for Mr. John Healy),
BEGS to announce that he has COMMENCED BUSINESS on his own account, and is prepared to supply BREAD and CAKES of superior quality at ruling prices.

NOTE THIS ADDRESS :—
Opposite Telegraph Office, Albion-street, 210 Warwick.

SAT 2 MARCH 1895. P3.

NOTICE.

THE undersigned wishes to notify to the general public that he has again secured the services of LOUIS OVERSTEAD, who is well known to be a First-class Baker, and who is now turning out FIRST-CLASS BREAD. He was for many years in charge of my baking business.
JOHN HEALY.
Guy-street, 1st July, 1899.   708

SAT 1 JUL 1899. P7. WA

Louis applied for 'naturalisation' on 1 August 1914, by which stage he was aged 48 and living in Pratten St, Warwick, with his wife, Annie Mary (née Jorgensen) and their five children, including their first son, Leslie Elliott ('Les') Overstead (born February 1892).

John Healy retired in 1916, leasing his business to Louis. While no record has been found of the duration of that lease, the *Warwick Daily News* carried announcements that L.E. Overstead had acquired the Palmerin St bakery of Daniel Maunsell (p. 70) following Maunsell's death in 1928.

The Overstead connection with the baking trade was to continue through Louis's son Les. While he had been a clerk throughout his working life, by 1934, aged 42, Les is listed in Electoral Rolls as a baker, having gone into business with his brother-in-law, Cyril Tucker.

To support this new enterprise, Henry Tucker built Derby House at 149 Palmerin St in 1935, the year before he died. It included accommodation for both families as well as a bakery shop and a state-of-the-art oven.

While Derby House was very much a Tucker initiative, the business was named L.E. Overstead and Co. to avoid confusion with Tucker Bros which was still a thriving business in King St, run by Norm and Alf Tucker.

With his clerical experience, Les undertook the office work for the new business and was also responsible for deliveries. Like his father and grandfather, Les's son, Gordon (born 1920) also went into the baking trade, working in both Warwick and Stanthorpe.

Louis Overstead died at the age of 89 on December 1954 in Cooroy where he lived towards the end of his life, assisting two of his daughters in the shop which they operated there. Almost exactly two years later, in December 1956, his son, Les, died at the age of 64.

The Oversteads' last link with the baking trade came within a couple of years of Les's death when Gordon, too, changed career direction, but a record of the family's ties to Warwick is in the columbarium wall in St Mark's Anglican Church which holds the ashes of Les, Claire and their son Gordon as well as three other members of the Overstead family.

Of the Tucker brothers, Leonard Charles Cyril ('Cyril') Tucker moved to the Gold Coast after the sale of the bakery to Fred Tanna, and died there in October 1971 at the age of 68. His older brother, Henry Norman Richings ('Norm') Tucker died in Warwick in July 1978, aged 79, followed by the last of the brothers, Alfred Richings ('Alf') Tucker in March 1990, aged 84. Both Norm and Alf are buried in Warwick Cemetery where their parents are also buried.

Alf's death in 1990 ended a family association with the baking trade in Warwick that had endured for 80 years.

Delivery vehicles in the yard at the rear of Derby House. The bakehouse was located on the left. (Photograph courtesy of Overstead family.)

Form A.

COMMONWEALTH OF AUSTRALIA.

NATURALIZATION ACT 1903.

APPLICATION FOR CERTIFICATE OF NATURALIZATION.

TO HIS EXCELLENCY THE GOVERNOR-GENERAL, No. of Certif. *15918*

1. **Name in full.** 1. I, *Louis Ellingson Overstead*

2. **Address and occupation.** of *Pratten-street, Warwick, Qld, Baker*

hereby apply for a Certificate of Naturalization under the *Naturalization Act 1903.*

3. **State "German subject" or "French citizen," &c., as case requires.** 2. I am by birth a² *Norwegian subject*

4. **Country of previous residence.** 3. I arrived in Australia from³ *Norway* on the _____ day of *May* in the year *1886*

5. **Name of ship.** per the⁴ *Garonne* and disembarked at the port of *Sydney.*

6. **State places, and periods in each.** 4. Since my arrival in Australia I have resided at⁵ *Warwick, Queensland. 28 years.*

5. I have resided in Australia continuously for a period of two years immediately preceding the date of this Application.

6. I forward herewith a Statutory Declaration, setting forth the particulars required by Section 6, Sub-section (1), paragraph (a) of the said Act.

7. **State whether married or unmarried, and residence of wife.** 7. I am⁶ *married and live with my wife at Pratten St. Warwick*

8. **State number.** 8. I have⁷ *five* children *two males and three females. Pratten-street, Warwick.*

9. **State number of each sex, and where resident.** 9. I am not a naturalized subject or citizen of any other country.

NOTE.—If the Applicant has taken out Naturalization Papers in any other country, this statement should be amended accordingly.

10. **State the name of the person, and whether he is a Justice of the Peace, Postmaster, Teacher of State School, or Officer of Police.** 10. I forward also a certificate signed by¹⁰ *Mr. B. J. De Conlay Justice of the Peace* to the effect that I am known to him, and am a person of good repute.

11. **Signature of applicant.** ¹¹ *L. E. Overstead*

Dated at *Warwick* the *1st August* 1914.

Louis Ellingson Overstead's Application for Certificate of Naturalisation (Ancestry.com).

Tucker family on the veranda of Derby House c. 1940. (Photograph courtesy of Matthew Collins.)

Derby House, 149 Palmerin St, October 2020. (Photograph courtesy of Eric Turner.)

The original veranda doors are behind the enclosed façade and other touches of the 1930s remain in the skylights and period furniture. (Author's photographs, September 2020.)

Although the bakehouse at the rear of Derby House has been demolished, access to the four flats on the upper floor is still via the stairs which were included in the design to enable the Tuckers and Oversteads to reach the bakehouse at night to mix the doughs and complete baking in time for morning deliveries and sales. (Author's photograph, September 2020.)

The Parker Family

The Parker family first became involved in the baking trade in Warwick in 1927 through Frederick Charles ('Fred') Parker. Apart from a decade in other Queensland centres, the family were to remain prominent in the industry in Warwick until the mid-1970s.

Parker's bakery was celebrated (and still remembered in 2020) for its unique creation – ice-cream buns. Consisting of a plain, sweet bun with a scoop of ice-cream inside, ice-cream buns cost threepence with a small, one-penny scoop, and sixpence with a larger, threepenny scoop. The buns were a great favourite of the St Mary's primary school pupils who would cross Palmerin St during 11.00 am recess for this special treat.

The Parker connection with Warwick began with Eli Parker who was born in Lincolnshire in the UK in 1865. Eli became a bootmaker, migrated to Australia at the age of 21, and initially set up business in Brisbane where he married American-born Elizabeth Gosland on Christmas Eve 1890.

Three children (Frederick, Jessie and Arthur) followed, as did a move to Warwick in 1897 where Eli quickly established his business and reputation in the district. By April 1911, he had opened Parker's Boot Warehouse in Palmerin St, just north of the Town Hall, and advertisements in the *Warwick Examiner and Times* and other newspapers indicate that the business continued to thrive.

> BOOTS and SHOES of every description, at all prices; Ladies at 3/6, 4/6, 7/6, 8/6, and upwards, Gents from 5/6 to 25/. Call and inspect.—PARKER'S BOOT WAREHOUSE, Palmerin-street.

SAT 30 DEC 1911. P8. WET

In August 1935, after almost 40 years in Palmerin St, Eli sold his bootmaking and repair business to Miss Ellen Rosina Quatermass[m] and started a new, smaller shoe shop in Plumbs Chambers in Fitzroy St. After his wife's death in 1943, he lived with his son, Fred, in the house next to the Palmerin St bakery, but continued to mend shoes in a shed at the rear of the bakery. Many Warwick

---

m   Miss Quatermass married in 1936 and continued the business in partnership with her husband, George Land Lowe until they sold it c. 1950 and left Warwick.

Parker's Boot Warehouse, Palmerin St on St George's Day, 23 April 1913. (Dornbusch family photograph from John Dean Collection, restored by Rolf Wood, courtesy of Máire Oakwood.)

SHOE SHOP CHANGES HANDS

Miss E. R. Quatermass announces by advertisement in this issue that she has purchased the old established business lately carried on by Mr. EW Parker. Miss Quatermass has had considerable experience in this line of business, having conducted stores in other centres. All leading lines will be carried, and patrons are invited to call and inspect the footwear offered.

FRI 9 AUG 1935. P7.

Eli Parker. (Photograph courtesy of Kay Quod.)

A young Fred Parker (left) with his good friend, Herbert Butler. (Photograph courtesy of Kay Quod.)

Rachel Shingles, Fred Parker's wife. (Photograph courtesy of Kay Quod.)

residents remember the rows of repaired shoes in his shed, neatly wrapped in brown paper and tied with string.

Widely respected as someone who was 'always the essence of courtesy and fair dealing to customers and competitors',[62] Eli became an Alderman in Warwick, was one of Australia's longest standing Freemasons, chaired the meeting held in 1908 to establish Warwick's Friendly Society, and was honoured for his contribution to the Oddfellows Lodge by a commemorative wall. He died on 6 December 1958 at the age of 93.

Eli's first son, Fred, was born in 1892 and had joined his father in the bootmaking trade by the age of nine. He continued in the trade in Warwick, marrying Rachel Shingles in February 1913, at the age of 20. The couple went on to have five children – Mona Edna, Beryl Jessie, Jack Frederick, Arthur Ray (known as both Ray and 'Curley'), and Douglas Bruce who died in Warwick in 1928 at the age of three years and five months.

During WWI and through the 1920s, Fred continued to work as a bootmaker, together with his brother Arthur, but by 1927, aged 35, he had made a dramatic career change.

A series of 40 small advertisements appeared in the *Catholic Advocate* from April 1927 to the same month the following year for 'Conley & Parker, high class bakers',[63] suggesting that Fred may have gone into business with Henry Alexander Conley, a young baker who was working in Warwick at the time.

No further record of the partnership has been found but, conjecture aside, it is known that Fred acquired the bakery at 41 Albion St because there is a record of his selling the business to Percy St Henry for £850.00 on 1 July 1931.[64] Over the next decade, he operated bakeries in a range of regional Queensland centres from Millmerran on the Darling Downs, to Cooroy and Cooran on the Sunshine Coast, Goomeri (near Kingaroy), and Mitchell in western Queensland, before returning to Warwick in 1938 and acquiring the Elseys building at 148 Palmerin St. The bakery turned out to be ideally located – parishioners attending Mass on Sundays at the Catholic church across the road quickly discovered the convenience of picking up their weekly bread orders after church.

Fred was known as 'a crack bike rider' and 'a footballer of great ability',[65] and had been a professional runner in his youth. He was also a foundation and later life member of the Warwick East Bowls Club. However, he is best remembered as a musician and bandsman.

Fred first began rehearsing with the Warwick town band under a pepperina tree as a nine-year-old in 1901, and went on to play cornet and euphonium with the band for almost 80 years, proudly wearing the light grey uniform with

Fred Parker was recognised in 1968 for his exceptional dedication to band music. (Photograph courtesy of Ray and Doreen Parker.)

its distinctive blue and gold stripe. He played under at least 18 bandmasters in his time with the band, often acting as bandmaster himself.

During WWII, he also played for the band established by the Queensland Echelon and Records Office of the Australian Army which operated from the Barnes building in Warwick for three years of the War, playing in the streets of Warwick every morning. His exceptional dedication as a bandsman in Warwick and in other Queensland centres, including Goondiwindi, was recognised in 1968 when he became the first Warwick bandsman to be honoured with the Queensland Band Association's Badge of Merit.

After the death of his wife, Rachel, in 1947, Fred was cared for by family members and by housekeepers. The first was Mrs Renee Williams, followed by Mrs Mary Maria Elizabeth Wilson who lived in a room above the shop at 148 Palmerin St from the early 1960s until the bakery business closed and the premises were sold. As she and Fred were almost the same age, this was a companionable arrangement for them both and they are remembered with great affection by family members and the many shop assistants who worked in the bakery.

Memories of Fred Parker and Mrs Wilson

'They always had a jar of butterscotch lollies on the table – I always got one.'
Gary Bonwick, Mrs Wilson's great-grandson

'They would always have morning tea with me. She made me tea and Mr Parker even gave me my own tea cup and saucer.'
Bonnie Carmichael, shop assistant 1974–76

'Mrs Wilson used to bring me a cup of tea for morning tea – with a 'bickie' on the side.'
Maureen Rolfe, shop assistant

By the time of his death in February 1982 at the age of 89, Fred had 24 grandchildren through his four children.

Fred's daughters both married bakers – Mona married Henry ('Harry') Byrnes in 1935 and Beryl married Athol ('Jim') Bright in 1937. While both men would work in the family bakery, as would Fred's son Jack, it was Harry who became most strongly identified with the business when Fred retired.

Mona and Harry had seven children: Michael ('Mick'), Fred, Genevieve, Vivienne, Maria, Paul, and Clare (always known as Monica) but Genevieve, aged not quite four years, was killed when run over by a wool truck at the family's bakery in Mitchell on 25 November 1942.

This tragedy was followed by the death in Warwick of Elizabeth,

Fred Parker's housekeeper, Mrs Mary Wilson, on her 90th birthday in 1982. She was born in Dungog NSW and lived for 60 years in Warwick until her death in May 1987. (Photograph by Col Furness, courtesy of Kay Quod.)

the Parker family matriarch, on 19 June 1943. As Fred also needed support in the bakery, Harry, Mona and their remaining six children returned to Warwick in 1945. Two years later, in 1947, Mona's mother Rachel died, and Mona herself died on 19 January 1952 at the age of just 38, shortly after the birth of her daughter, Clare.

The response of the Parker and Byrnes families to these life-changing events was pragmatic. Harry arranged for his youngest son, Paul, to be adopted by a Byrnes family member in Mitchell and for baby Clare to be cared for by Mona's best friend, Zilla Drew. Zilla and her husband Roy formally adopted Clare when she was two or three years old, always calling her Monica (her second name) to avoid confusion with the Drews' adopted daughter, Clare.

Harry also put Vivienne and Maria into boarding school in Warwick, while the two older boys, Mick and Fred, continued their schooling as day students. In 1956, he married Mary Kreibke and had two further children with her: Harry John ('John') and Ann. Harry died in Brisbane at the age of 97, surviving Mary by just over eight months. He is buried in the Mount Gravatt cemetery.

Harry Byrnes and Zilla Drew (circled) were both champion tennis players. Zilla raised Monica Byrnes following the death of Harry's wife, Mona. (Haig Studio photograph courtesy of Catherine Byrnes.)

Fred's second son-in-law, Athol ('Jim') Bright, was born in 1913 in Millmerran where his father was a storekeeper. In March 1936, when Athol was in his early twenties, his father was declared bankrupt and died in March the following year. In Millmerran, Athol had come to know Fred Parker and his family and, the month before his father died, he married Fred's daughter, Beryl Jessie. They went on to have eight children (Donald, Barry, Robert, Kevin John, Patricia, Margaret, Ross, and Catherine).

During WWII, Athol served in the Citizen Military Forces and in the AIF, and after the war he worked for his father-in-law in Warwick as a baker until the late 1950s when he left Warwick suddenly. He died in Braidwood (near Queanbeyan, NSW) in 1972. Beryl remained in Warwick for some years and died in 2004.

Jack Frederick, the eldest of Fred's three sons, served in WWII and worked for his father as a baker in Warwick in the late 1940s. He then became an engine driver, first in Pittsworth in 1954 and then in Toowoomba from 1958. He lived with his wife Alice Joyce ('Joyce') and their two children, Warren and Robyne, and died in 1997.

Fred's youngest son, Arthur Ray ('Ray'), succeeded in avoiding the baking trade altogether. Born in 1930, Ray joined the Army in 1951 and married Doreen Neal in 1953. They went on to have seven children and, for a total of 26 years, lived on Army bases in Townsville, Brisbane, Inverbrackie (South Australia) and Melbourne as well as being posted for two and a half years from July 1963 to what was then Malaya. It was during his time in the Army that Ray was nicknamed 'Curley' in reference to the much-loved WWII cartoon characters, Bluey and Curley (see p.166). At the end of his army service in 1977, 'Curley' returned to Warwick where he worked as caretaker at Warwick Town Hall until he finally retired. In 2020, he and Doreen, both nonagenarians, were still living independently in Warwick.

By 2020, the descendants of Eli Parker and Elizabeth Gosland numbered well over a hundred, all of them proud of the contribution the Parker family made to Warwick over a period of more than 80 years through the bootmaking and bakery trades, band music, sport, a wide range of community organisations – and especially the invention of ice-cream buns!

Henry Tucker and the Tucker Brothers

Henry Tucker in his Mason's regalia and Mary-Ann in Derby, UK, with four of their eight children. (Photographs courtesy of Tucker family.)

Henry Tucker was born 2 June 1863, in the village of Fairlight, near Hastings on the south coast of England where his father, Charles, was a schoolmaster, teaching mainly the children of the coastguards.

When Henry was still young, Charles was appointed to a Church of England School in Bedfordshire. It was here that he fell into a fire, disfiguring his face and blinding him in the right eye. The family then moved to Ropsley near Grantham in Lincolnshire where Henry spent his boyhood before being apprenticed to a baker and grocer in Grantham. After following both trades for some years, he went into business himself in Derby where he met Mary Ann Radford (born 1866), possibly through her brother, Charles, who was also a baker and who had premises in Leonard St, Derby.

Henry and Mary Ann were married on 6 June 1892 in St Luke's Church, Derby, and eight children quickly arrived: Claire (1893), Ethel 'Mikey' (1895), Lilian (1896), Norman (1898), Dorothy 'Dorrie' (1902), Cyril (1903), Alf (1906), and Mary (1909).

Business in Derby was a struggle, and after 20 years, Henry decided to explore prospects in Australia. He arrived in Brisbane on 15 July 1910, on the *Everton Grange,* together with his eldest daughters Claire and Lilian, and eldest son, Norman.

For reasons unknown, Henry decided to settle in Warwick where he took what he described as 'a boy's job' as a carter at 25 shillings a week with Guy St baker, John Healy, in order to earn enough to be able to bring the rest of his family from Derby to join him. His wife and the remaining five children lived with Mary Ann's parents, Leonard and Sarah Radford, in Byron St, Derby until 8 April 1911 when Mary Ann, together with Mikey, Dorrie, Cyril, Alf and Mary, left London on the *Norseman*, arriving in Brisbane on 22 May 1911.

By 1914, after three years with Healy, Henry was able to go into business for himself, establishing Tucker's Hygienic Bakery at 32A King St.[n] Norm, Alf and Cyril all learned their trade there and in 1923 Henry signed an agreement with all three of them and it became Henry Tucker and Sons.

In 1927, the three brothers purchased the King St bakery from their father and renamed it Tucker Bros. In 1931, it passed into the hands of two of the brothers (Norm and Alf) while the third brother, Cyril, went into partnership with his brother-in-law, Les Overstead. (Les had married Henry's eldest daughter Claire in 1916).

The new undertaking was supported by Henry Tucker and operated as L.E. Overstead and Co. to distinguish it from the Tucker Bros bakery in King St.

The nearby Palmerin St bakery of Daniel Maunsell had been acquired by L.E. Overstead in 1928, but in 1935, Henry built Derby House and its associated bakehouse, shop and accommodation at 149 Palmerin St. The business became Warwick Bakery with Cyril, Les and their families living above the shop and the Tanna family (p. 141) later occupying another of the four flats, creating lifelong friendships between the children of the three families.

When Les left the business and moved to Brisbane, Cyril purchased it from him and continued to operate it as Warwick Bakery until early 1950 when it was sold to Fred Tanna. During the same period, Norm and Alf had continued to run the King St bakery as Tucker Brothers. They did this until May 1951 when, due to Norm's ill health, the business was sold to Mervyn Willett.

The relationship between the Tucker family and the Warwick community was a strong one, in part because of Henry's values as a committed Mason which led him to share the success of his business with the community as well as with his family.

He was elected as a member of the Warwick Town Council in 1933 and in addition to the family home, *The Elms*, Henry purchased many houses in Warwick and made them available to families at reasonable rent. In 1924, he paid the passage to Australia for his wife's youngest brother, Alfred Radford, together with his wife Amy Winifred and their infant daughter, Amy.

Henry and Mary Ann also returned to England for a visit during which he arranged for his father's home in Ropsley to be connected to a water supply –

---

n   Trading as 'H. Tucker and Son'. Accommodation and an office were on ground level behind the shop. On the left was a driveway leading to the bakery where delivery vehicles were loaded. See image p. 90.

the first house in the village to have such a connection.

The impact of Henry's childhood accident remained with him throughout his life – he chose not to pursue a career as a teacher because he feared the effect his disfigurement may have had on impressionable children. He also wore glasses with a smoked lens over the right eye and always preferred to be photographed so that only the left side of his face could be seen. The photograph below is a rare exception.

Henry died in 1936 at the age of 73. Mary Ann followed him in 1948. Both are buried in the Warwick cemetery.

Henry Tucker (centre) in Warwick council chambers in 1933. (Photograph from author's collection.)

Mary Ann ('Polly') Tucker at her desk. (Photograph from author's collection.)

The Tucker family home, *The Elms*, cnr Albion and Percy Sts, Warwick.
(Author's photographs, 2012.)

Aerial photograph of King St, Warwick in 1929 showing location of Tucker's Bakery opposite His Majesty's (later King's) Theatre and with the Barnes Building on the corner with Palmerin St. (Image sourced from Picture Queensland, State Library of Queensland.)

Graves of Henry and Mary Ann Tucker, Warwick Cemetery.
(Author's photograph, 2018.)

DELIVERY AND DISTRIBUTION

The first bread deliveries to shops and homes in Warwick were made exclusively by horse-drawn carts – except for an occasional bicycle.

While motorised vehicles were progressively introduced, advertisements for cart horses were still appearing in the *Warwick Daily News* in the early 1950s, and while various innovations were introduced to improve the efficiency, comfort and safety of carts, they always had one unpredictable element – the horse.

Stories of accidents and near misses abound.

While a cart horse ending in the Condamine in 1934[66] and a spectacular display in the main street in 1939[67] were sufficiently newsworthy to be reported (see p. 92), every baker knew that a simple gust of wind could result in a bolting horse, a scattered load, costly repairs and injury to both horse and driver. Horses were also known to take advantage of open gates, creating interruptions to deliveries that were not quickly rectified.[68]

In addition to their unpredictability, horses needed to be stabled, fed, watered and shod and this required storage for fodder, space for a yard and stables, and the services of farriers, vets and saddlers.

Carters were the public relations staff of the baking trade and needed a high level of interpersonal skills to deal with customers' expectations. They also needed to be reliable, punctual, able to work hard – and prepared to deal with horses.

HORSE PLUNGES INTO RIVER.

Dragging behind it a light baker's delivery cart, a horse dashed along a street in East Warwick, about 7.30 o'clock yesterday morning, and finished by plunging into the Condamine River. Fortunately the cart did not capsize, otherwise the horse might have been drowned. On the contrary, the extraordinary sight was witnessed of the horse swimming with the cart floating behind, the top just showing above the water. As the horse swam near the bank Ralph Brown (15), the lad who had been driving the cart for his father, pluckily waded into the river, fully clothed, and, with the water up to his armpits, released the horse from the shafts. Subsequently a motor truck was requisitioned to drag the cart from the muddy river bed. The horse had bolted from near the corner of Fitzroy and East streets, the strap round the wheel having come undone while Brown was delivering bread to a customer. Fortunately there were only about 30 loaves in the cart when it made its plunge into the river.

WED 18 JULY 1934. P4. WDN

Baker's Horse Bolts

Cart Capsizes After Striking Three Cars

Morning shoppers in Palmerin-street yesterday were treated to a first class display of rodeo thrills when a horse attached to a baker's van and standing opposite the Town Hall took fright and bolted. Veering round and galloping on the wrong side of the street towards the Byrne monument, the bolting horse crashed the cart against three cars parked in a row between the Q.N. Bank and L. B. Eastwell's premises. The third collision turned the cart over on to its side and the horse, probably feeling the extra weight behind it, promptly decided to call the whole thing off and stood still while bystanders righted the cart and the driver took charge again.

SAT 1 JUL 1939. P2.

Lost and Found

LOST Grey Cart Horse, branded 1ZY; also Brown Cart Horse, unbranded, star and snip, hogged mane. £1 reward for information leading to recovery of same. Ring 727 or reply Clarke & Glasby, Warwick.

SAT 13 DEC 1947. P10.

Martin Brown in the cart he designed and built in 1938. (Photograph from author's collection.)

Wally Siebuhr. (Photograph courtesy of Ted Siebuhr.)

Wally Siebuhr was one of the many bread, milk and ice carters who operated in and around Warwick until the mid-1950s. His story is included as a tribute to those many boys and men (no women carters have been identified in Warwick to date°) who formed the vital link between the baker and the customer in the time before supermarkets and large-scale commercial bakeries.

A—W. SIEBUHR. Butter and Ice Delivery to all parts of town. Satisfaction assured. Phone 233.

WED 8 NOV 1939. P8.

Wallace William Siebuhr, universally known as 'Wally', was the first of eight children. Born in Rockhampton in 1912, he moved to Warwick with his parents and siblings when he was young and remained there until his death in 1982 at the age of 70.

Wally married Beatrice Shelley in 1936 and they had three sons – James, Edward and Raymond. James died in 1958 at the age of 20 after being hit by a car when riding his bike. Ted and Ray went on to successful careers, Ted as an educator and Ray as a public servant and government lawyer.

As a child, Wally had contracted osteomyelitis, a rare but debilitating bone infection which was to cause him severe back and leg pain throughout his life. Despite this disability, he enlisted in the Army on 30 April 1942 and, while his health precluded him from overseas service, he served as a Private in 9 Works Company in Australia until discharged on 19 December 1945.

Wally had operated his own butter and ice delivery business before WWII and went on to serve the Warwick community for many years after the war as a bread carter, working for both Lloyd and Harry Crone from their Grafton St bakery and for Rex and Lyla French in King St.

The collaborative competition that operated among the bakers meant that Wally was also well known in all the bakehouses of that time – if a dough failed or supplies ran short for whatever reason, bakeries would always support one another, despatching a carter to pick up or deliver items.

In the era before motorised delivery vehicles, Wally, like all carters, developed an efficient partnership with his cart horse which followed the delivery route with no instruction beyond an occasional whistle.

The families of bakery staff were customarily supplied with free, oven-fresh bread and, as for most 'bakery children', the aroma of the bakehouse remains an indelible memory for both of Wally's sons, as does accompanying their father on delivery rounds. Ted, as a student teacher, also worked in the Grafton St bakery during university holidays.

Wally's transition to a Holden panel van in the 1950s was not without incident, especially when his sons discovered that the vehicle could be unlocked by rocking it, and started simply by reaching under the dashboard and pushing a sixpence horizontally between the two terminals at the rear of the press-button starter.

o The idea of women carters was dismissed as 'a passing fancy' when proposed in 1942 by the Associated Bread Manufacturers to relieve the WWII shortage of male workers. (*Warwick Daily News* 1942, 29 September, p. 3.)

Daniel Maunsell, Baker and Confectioner, Warwick, c. 1900. (John Oxley Library, State Library of Queensland Neg. No: 102507.)

Carters and their horses in the yard at the rear of Brown's Bakery, 41 Albion St. Date and carters unknown. (Photograph from author's collection.)

Carters and their delivery rigs were photographed on more than one occasion on the street outside Haig's Photographic Studio. (Photograph of Jack Clifford in an Overstead rig courtesy of Brian Clifford; unknown carter in Tucker's Bakery rig below.)

Wanted to Buy

WANTED Cart Horse. No crocks. Apply Brown's Bakery.

WED 15 APR 1953. P6.

Situations Vacant

BREAD Carter wanted. Horse drawn vehicle. Apply Clarke and Glasby, Grafton Street.

FRI 5 DEC 1952. P6.

Advertisements related to horse-drawn deliveries still appeared in the *Warwick Daily News* in the 1950s.

The six-wheeled delivery outfit invented and built by Martin Brown for country deliveries in 1939. Unknown driver and location. (Photograph courtesy of Pauline Peel.)

In the early twentieth century, several of the small towns around Warwick (e.g. Allora, Clifton, Killarney, Tannymorel, Yangan) had their own successful bakeries, but the introduction of motorised vehicles from the 1930s meant that Warwick bakers could easily deliver bread to farms, villages and towns within a 48 km radius of the town. The Brown's Bakery route (p. 97) is typical.

The country delivery round was one of the toughest jobs for carters. In his memoirs, Ralph Brown described his 'second job' as a bread carter while working as a baker for his father in the 1940s. His experiences were by no means unique.

> In my second job as bread-carter, I did the country run through a 30-mile radius of Warwick, covering about 600 miles a week. I drove the Ford Blitz truck for the Bread Distributing Company with a bread box on the tray which held up to 400 loaves. I delivered about 1500 loaves each week, from Monday to Friday. To defray costs, I also used to pick up and deliver papers, meat from butchers, even parcels from shops.
>
> The roads were very bad with corrugations and little bitumen. I well recall putting the Blitz into low gear, putting on chains and grinding across black soil roads for miles. There was no need to steer – the wheels followed the tracks of the previous vehicle.
>
> I have been caught in deep water which cut out the ignition and when the only way to get across was to put the gears in low and use the

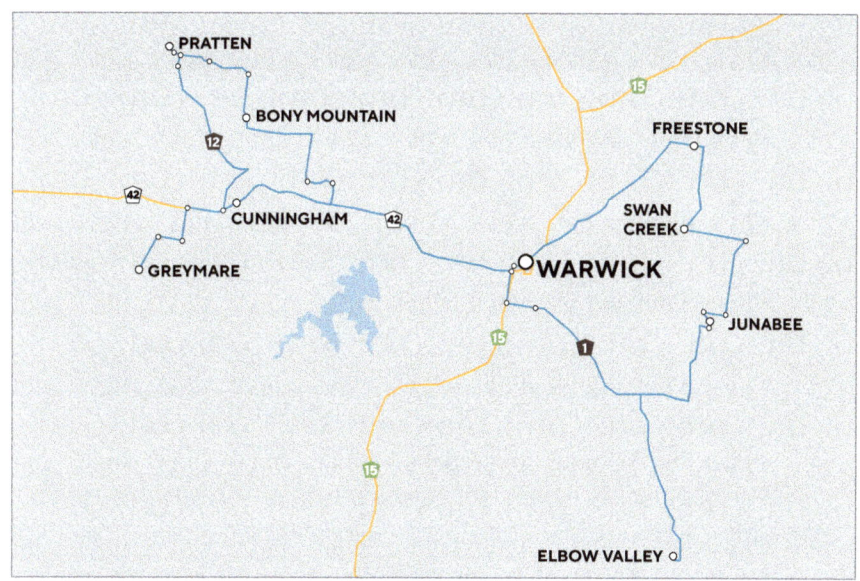

Brown's Bakery's daily country delivery run c. 1940.

crank handle to wind the truck onto high ground. This was the hardest of jobs involving crawling under the truck, removing the distributor on the cam shaft, drying it out, and then keeping going.

One bitterly cold day in July, just on dark, I was about to make the last delivery of the run to Mrs Conway at Willowvale when I just fell asleep at the wheel. I hadn't slept the night before because I had been up all night baking, and I had taken the door off the bread truck to speed up the job, so it was pretty cold.

Fortunately, Mrs Conway saw me slumped over the wheel and the next thing I remember was her waking me up and her son Dennis helping me into their warm kitchen. Mrs Conway gave me a stiff hot rum and lemon, thawed me out, and made me stay until I was OK. If there is an earthly heaven, that was it. I have the greatest respect for the Irish Catholics – they are the kindest of people.

Maree Read recalls an occasion when the Conway family's kindness was repaid:

One time when Ralph Brown was delivering bread, he arrived at my Gran's home in Victoria St. When she didn't answer at the front door, he went around the back and found she had taken a fall the previous *afternoon and had lain on cold concrete all night. As it was winter and the houses were closed up, the neighbours had not heard her calling for help. Others had to wait for their delivery while Mr Brown organised the ambulance, contacted family, etc. Gran broke both wrists but didn't even get a cold. I still say, 'Thank you, Mr Brown'.*

Another 'bakery child', Desmond ('Bill') Overstead, still remembers the experience of going with his father, Les, to the farms and shops in the district on their delivery round in the late 1930s:

We would literally 'break bread' (usually a Tin Loaf, still warm) and eat it under a tree. Dad loved matured cheese, so we carried a large portion to eat with the bread. People did not carry water with them everywhere in those days. We would ask for a drink of water at a farm, and would be given an old enamel mug, or a 'dipper' of tank water. I still think the smell of freshly baked bread is one of the best smells possible. I would get that smell in the back of the van, and in the 'Tin Room' where freshly baked loaves, still in their tins, would be placed to cool.

When motorised vehicles were introduced, the versatility of utilities quickly made them popular.

A 'bread box' could be slid into the tub of the 'ute' for deliveries but removed if the vehicle was needed for other purposes. The Brown's Bakery ute shown on page 99 was acquired c. 1960 and was the last of the series of hard-working Holdens that served the bakery (and the Brown family) between 1952 and 1966 when the business was sold to Joe and Mary Hall.

Michael Carter remembers a period during his apprenticeship with Rex French in the early 1960s when there was a protracted problem with the oven at the King St bakery. The solution was to line the tub of the bakery ute with flour bags, load in the mixed dough, then drive 30 km to Tannymorel where it was rested, 'tinned up' and baked by arrangement with the local baker. When cool, the bread was carted back to Warwick to be delivered.

Given that carts were essential for bread deliveries and subject to a great deal of wear and tear, coachbuilders were a key companion trade for bakers in the era of horse-drawn deliveries, and contact between the two trades was frequent and inevitable.

In the case of the Tucker family, that business contact became a family connection when one of the Tucker daughters, Ethel May, married Arthur Ernest Flitcroft, a member of one of Warwick's earliest coachmaking families. Arthur's father, John Thomas Flitcroft, had learned the trade from his older half-brother, William, and acquired the Warwick Coach Works in Grafton St in

Photograph courtesy of Overstead family.

Photograph from author's collection.

Household delivery by T.W. Lawrence and Co. at McEvoy St, Warwick in 1960s. Unidentified carter. (Photograph courtesy of Sharon Lingard.)

1909, while William continued to operate the Pioneer Coach Works in Albion St. John Thomas was born in Brisbane, but William had arrived in Australia with his parents in 1863 and, after serving his apprenticeship, travelled to Warwick in 1874 by bullock wagon. The 20-year-old William found work in W. Hurford's Pioneer Coach Works, later becoming manager of the business. In 1896, he purchased the Albion St coach works from Hurford and operated it from then on under the Flitcroft name. One of William's sons, John William, took over the business in 1928 and three other sons (Seth Charles, William Daniel and Harold Arthur) also worked in the trade. As typically happened with coachworks at the time, both businesses transitioned to work on motor vehicles.

**THE WARWICK COACH WORKS,
Grafton-street.**

JOHN T. FLITCROFT
Begs to notify that he has Purchased the Coachbuilding Business recently conducted by R. Johnson, in Grafton-street, and hopes to receive a share of public patronage.
All work entrusted to my care will have my best attention.

MON 30 AUG 1909. P4.

William Flitcroft's coachworks display at the Warwick Exhibition Building in 1904.
(Image sourced from Picture Queensland, State Library of Queensland.)

The coach factory of John Thomas Flitcroft in Grafton St, c. 1923.
(Image sourced from Picture Queensland, State Library of Queensland.)

TOOLS OF THE TRADE

In 1948, Siegfried Giedion produced a comprehensive and influential book about mechanisation and its impact on daily life. In it, he claimed that the baking oven deserved to be ranked, alongside the axe and the knife, as 'a basic tool of human inventory' and 'the product of unfathomably ancient experience'.[69]

The classic wood-fired oven was certainly the most fundamental and widespread item of equipment in Australian bakeries until the era of mass-produced bread in the mid-twentieth century, and that particular style of brick oven, with forged iron fittings, is still referred to as a 'Scotch' oven.

Scotch ovens were typically some two metres high, four metres wide and five metres deep. The enclosed baking cavity was significantly smaller with an arched ceiling or 'crown' about a metre from the floor or 'sole' of the oven. The whole was made of brick or stone, encased by several tonnes of heat-retaining sand above and below, with the outer walls held together by metal tie rods. The drawing on page 103 shows the construction in cross-section and the photograph on the same page of the nineteenth-century bakery which once stood at 41 Albion St, Warwick, shows the wooden sleepers used to secure the tie rods and reinforce the structure.

According to Australian cultural historian, Roger Haden, 'precisely how, why or from what date the term *Scotch oven* was coined remains uncertain'.[70] Nevertheless, they represented what he calls 'the pinnacle of nineteenth-

Illustration © John Hodgson (www.johnhodgson.uk.com) of the Scotch oven at Llynon Bakery, Wales, produced for an explanatory reconstruction for an on-site information board, made for the Gwynedd Archaeological Trust.

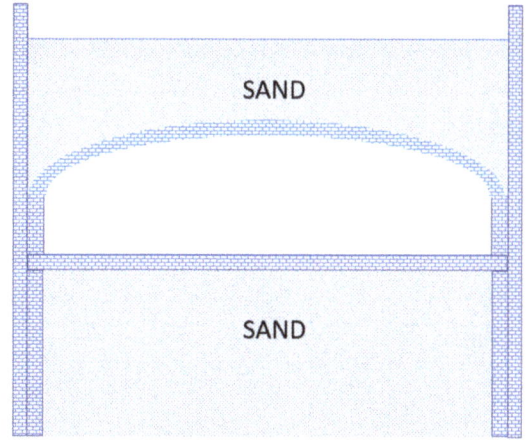

Drawing of oven cross-section courtesy of Michael Carter.

The bakehouse wall at 41 Albion St, showing reinforcement. (Author's photograph, 1998.)

century commercial oven engineering' and were almost universal in country towns throughout the UK in the last decades of that century.

It was a small, natural step for the Scotch oven to arrive in Australia with the many Scots who immigrated, with the result that most of these ovens were built between 1850 and 1910. As Roger Haden says, 'Since that time, many, perhaps most, have either been bulldozed or lie disused in various stages of disintegration'.[71] This is certainly the case in Warwick where there are no remaining Scotch ovens of that era in operation.

Firing a Scotch oven is a skill in itself.

A wood-fired oven needs to run for c. three days for the bricks and encasing sand to absorb the necessary heat. Wood is then burned for c. 10 additional hours to take the temperature to its maximum. At that point, the fire is 'killed' and the oven allowed to drop back to baking temperature.

Oil-fired ovens were much simpler – and took a significantly shorter time. Michael Carter explains:

> *To fire the oven, a yeast wrapper (or other waxed paper) was lit and put into the firebox. The valve on the oil burner was then turned on slightly and the burner swung into position with the nozzle in the firebox. The big blower was then turned on and, once the oil had caught alight, a lever on the burner was opened slightly until burning oil was being blown into the firing chamber. More oil and air were then added progressively until the blower was fully open. The oil was then trimmed to burn clean with no soot. To turn the burner off, the oil valve was wound closed. A loud 'WHHHHUUUTTTT' sound signalled that the flame had gone out. The air could then be turned off and the burner swung away from the firebox.*

Firing the oven was only the first step. Traditional bakers needed to develop an intuitive understanding of the physics and chemistry involved in the baking process if they were to be successful:

> *To cook many loaves of bread at once initially requires a hot oven (230°C). Once hot, the brickwork emits a constant radiant heat for many hours, even if the heat source has been removed. Crucially, the crown maximises the top heat available for cooking. When a mass of proved [risen]…bread dough is introduced into the hot oven, the coolness (and moistness) of the damp dough immediately begins to lower the interior air temperature of the oven chamber. Gradually, however, the heat reserve in the bricks begins to steadily raise the temperature again. The yeast within the bread dough…now once again leavens the dough, bringing the loaves to their maximum height before the intense heat finally kills the yeast and sets the crust. The moisture released by the loaves of dough during baking to some extent accumulates in the oven, ensuring the crispness of the bread's crust. Once formed, the crust also protects the moistness of the bread's porous open interior, preventing the loaf from becoming too dry.[72]*

Given that the oven was the most fundamental element of a bakery, it is not surprising that G.B. McInnes, when he opened his new Palmerin St bakery in 1918, adopted the newest technology. The advertorial published in the *Warwick Examiner and Times* on 16 January that year provides a fascinating level of detail about the Allan's Patent Steel Oven which he installed:

This massive structure, which is throughout composed of solid steel, is a great acquisition to the baking trade, and possesses many pronounced advantages over the more common brick oven. One of the chief advantages of the steel oven, which has a capacity of 400 loaves at the one operation, is the rapidity with which the oven can be heated. In regard to the production of bread another great feature is the retention of the steam in the baking process. The oven is so faithfully manufactured as to be perfectly airtight, and the consequence is that the baked article contains considerably more moisture than the product which comes out of the brick oven. Hence, too, the correct weight of the loaf of bread is positively assured to customers. Considerable economy in the matter of fuel is also a noteworthy feature, and a saving of upward of 30 per cent per annum can easily be effected in this respect. The new baking apparatus is fitted with a patent pyrometer, and the original price of these steel ovens is £375. The pyrometer proves of great assistance to the operating baker, and enables him to ascertain the temperature for all classes of work, and ensures uniformity in the produced article. The dimensions of this oven (outer casing) are 15ft. x 14ft 6in., and the internal measurements (or those of the inner oven proper) are 10ft. x 11ft., while the height of the steel structure is 7ft. Before erection the weight of the oven is 8 tons, but after having been set in by the company's expert, it is estimated that its total weight would be about 50 tons. The tremendous weight is accounted for by the extraordinarily large amount of sand which is absolutely essential in the building of the oven.

Allen's, an American company, were evidently quite aggressive in marketing their ovens. The impressive display stand in the photograph on page 106 was erected by Mauri Bros and Thomson at the Royal Easter exhibition in Sydney in May 1908 where, according to the accompanying newspaper article,[73] the ovens were fired and produced frequent batches of 'scones, cakes, etc.'. The company claimed that, by that date, they had installed 20 bakery ovens in Australia.

Traditional Scotch ovens may have had the same basic design, but each had its individual quirks, and bakers needed to become skilled at managing the process of producing different products. Bread was baked first, then buns and pastry and finally cake as the oven cooled. Because of this, pastrycooks started work later and some bakers would even give the oven a small firing while the cake was being prepared if it had cooled too much.

As the temperature of these ovens was not readily controlled, the practice of cross-trading developed in Warwick and other communities, with some bakers making only cake but buying in bread from other bakeries for sale to their customers. Michael Carter cites one example:

EXHIBITED BY MAURI BROS. & THOMPSON.

Merv. Willett only had electric Deck ovens. Their volume was limited but they had great, stable temperature, so he made cake and buns but bought in bread from other bakeries. Cross-trading enabled other bakeries to have cake in their display cases, and bread bakers would often buy in trays of cake which were cut and dipped to make lamingtons.

Oil-fired ovens made life easier as firing could be done for as long as required, even a short 10-minute firing, but the relationship between bakers and their ovens remained critical and surprisingly intimate as seen in this quote from an oven restorer:

Another joyful weekend working on the oven. The first job was to remove the cast iron damper used to regulate the air flow in the chimney. The combination of rust, a century of chimney dust and fallen bricks had locked the damper firmly in place. Up until now I have been very careful with the old oven, gently repairing what I could, but the stuck damper called for some brute force. A combination of a crowbar, some blocks of wood and a metal hook did the job. With the damper removed the next job was to sweep and clean the chimney, then return the damper, with the rust removed. And now for the most exciting part of the weekend – it was time to begin a light firing of the oven, starting the slow process of removing the moisture. A baker friend of mine who also has a lovely old Scotch oven said that when you first fire these ovens after years of neglect, they 'cry'. Sure enough the oven did cry, oh so gently, as moisture began to weep from the bricks and iron. Who knew that the relationship between a baker and his oven could become so personal and emotional?[74]

A similar experience is described by Michael Carter who re-fired a dormant oven at Parker's Palmerin St bakery in the mid-1970s. Parker's had ceased baking their own bread, but sold bread from French's bakery in the shop while using the bakehouse for storage.

When I started my business in 1974, I approached Fred Parker about leasing the bakery. We checked that the crown was still intact and, as the oven was still in great nick, he agreed to lease the bakery to me, provided that the oven survived a firing. I did this over a number of days starting with a small fire of newspapers inside the oven, then a small timber fire, gently bringing it up to a full fire in the firebox. The oven crown survived and we baked a small batch in it.

In addition to the ovens, the other essential tools of the trade included troughs into which the mixed dough was tipped and allowed to prove (rise).

The word 'trough' was pronounced variously in different parts of Australia and the world, but the Warwick baking community always pronounced it to rhyme with 'dough'. The hip-high troughs were made of wood and could be separated into sections by removable dividers. The troughs also had removable wood covers which were used as a work bench to weigh and shape the loaf-sized pieces of dough.

With increasing mechanisation and new technologies in bread ovens, traditional wooden troughs are now rarely seen, but they have left their mark on the history of the trade through their association with 'rope'.

'Rope' is the common name for *Bacillus subtilis* and several other bacteria that can spoil batch after batch of bread. Rope was dreaded by all bakers and could even result in bakery closures. Generally worse in summer and in conditions of high humidity, rope can survive high baking temperatures and is difficult to eradicate. Michael Carter recalls:

The bread looks fine when it comes out of the oven, but by the time it has cooled, the crumb is discoloured and sticky. When separating married loaves, instead of white sheets of crumb, there would be long, brown, slimy *strands (rope). As a kid I helped my father wash down a bakery which had not been in use for some time as a precaution. All timber surfaces, troughs, trough lids, benches, etc. had to be washed with vinegar, and walls had to be repainted. Following this, a product known as Sentinal (I think it was lactic acid) was used to wash surfaces and equipment and was added in small concentrations to doughs until the bakery could be thoroughly cleaned. One solution was to line the troughs with tinned steel, as joins in timber troughs were prone to harbouring the bacteria. Prior to the introduction of lined troughs, wooden joins and joints had to be soaked heavily in vinegar to kill the bacteria but this was often only successful for a short period.*

'Trough' and other terminology of the trade was brought to the attention of the public of Warwick in 1934 through a court case. Martin Brown had successfully sought damages from Walter Percy St Henry for misrepresenting the volume of sales when he had purchased the Albion St bakery from St Henry the previous year. The court report in The *Warwick Daily News* on 3 February included the following lesson:

When witnesses in a case in the magistrate's court at Warwick this week began to talk of 'bucket' and 'dipper' measurements, laymen present in court were given a new lesson in mensuration. The baker witnesses were talking in terms common to their own metier, but which are conundrums to the majority of persons outside the baking trade. A furrow of puzzlement even passed across the usually placid brow of the police magistrate when 'buckets' and 'dippers' were first mentioned. It was explained that the number of loaves of bread that might be turned out from any particular batch was estimated not on the quantity of flour used, but on the number of buckets or dippers of water used in making the dough. With one 'bucket' about 46 two-pound loaves are the generally accepted output, while a 'dipper' is the equivalent of seven two-pound loaves. Another trade puzzler confronted Mr Knyvett [the Magistrate] when, on perusing a book showing the output of a particular bakery, he came across an entry marked 'married loaves'. These 'married loaves' really had no connubial significance, but, it was explained, were merely trade terms for the large double tin loaves.

In addition to the mysteries of troughs, buckets and dippers, there was the process of 'burning-in' new bread tins. As Michael Carter explains:

Bakers 'greased' new tins by dipping a piece of flour bag or a rag into an old bread tin of cheap vegetable oil such as rapeseed. The greased tins were then loaded into the oven at the end of the day's baking to be 'burned in'. If tins were used new without burning-in, the bread would stick and the crust would tear when the loaves were 'knocked out'.

(Author's photograph, February 2021, Miles Historical Village Museum.)

Two other essential items used in bakehouses were the scuffle and the peel.

The scuffle was essentially a mop – often a wet cloth on the end of a peel handle. It was used to clean ash from the floor of wood-fired ovens. The illustration (p. 102) shows a scuffle as well as the forged iron oven door, the reinforcing tie rods, the firebox, and a peel.

The peel enables items to be inserted and removed from the oven. Traditionally made of wood so that it did not over-heat and ignite or create the risk of burns, the word appears to derive from the French *pelle* (shovel). As Michael Carter explains:

> *Bakers decided among themselves who would 'peel' and who would 'knock out', and often swapped duties for each batch. If there were enough bakers, sometimes a third baker was the 'stacker', packing the loaves onto metal racks which were often wheeled outside to cool before slicing. Sometimes, large electric fans were used in the bakery on big production days to speed up the process.*

The layout of bakeries was dictated by the need for efficiency and so tended to be very similar. Michael Carter has drawn from memory the plan (p. 110) of the bakery at 32A King St as it was when he worked there as a boy in the 1960s.

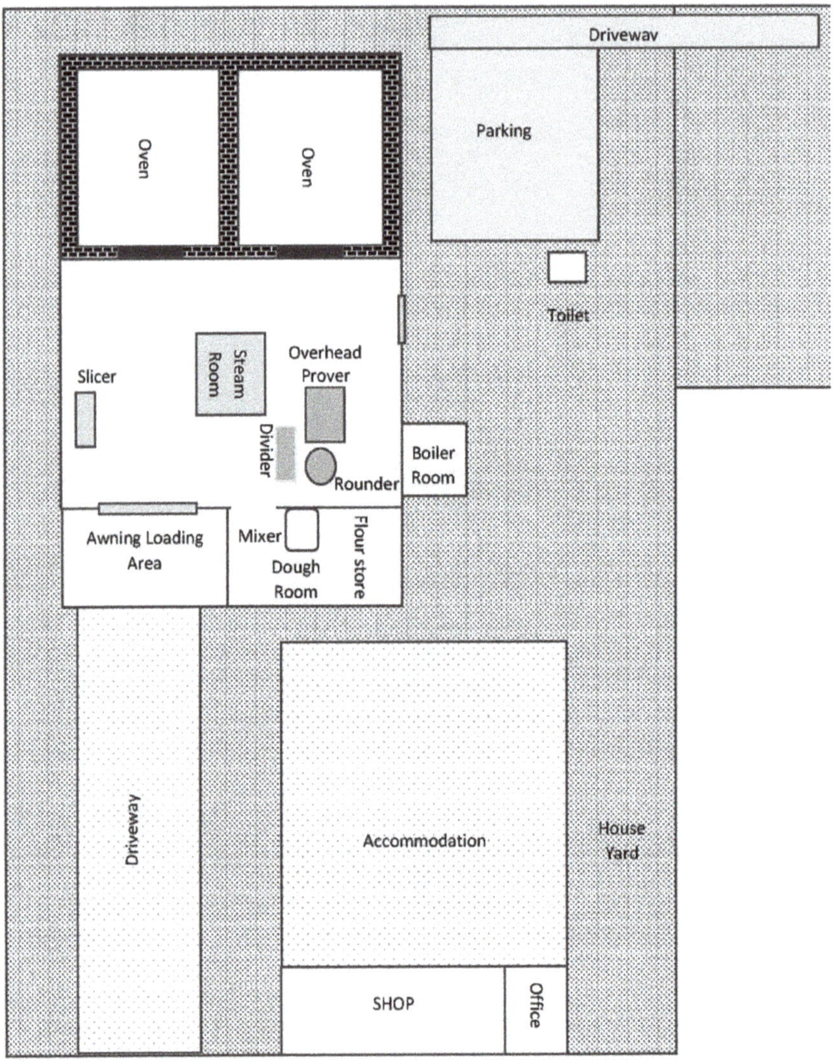

Tucked away behind a compactus in what is now a storeroom, this iron firebox door is the only remaining evidence that there was once a bakery at 148 Palmerin St. (Author's photograph, September 2020.)

Bakers Frank Lawrence (L) and Neville Matthews, c. 1969. (Photograph courtesy of Michael Carter.)

THE CHEMISTRY AND ALCHEMY OF BREAD

By the 1950s, bread manufacturing had barely crossed the threshold from domestic to commercial production, so most bread in Warwick was still made by hand, as it had been since the first bakers arrived almost a century beforehand. It was produced with minimal mechanical assistance, baked in temperamental ovens, and bakers still relied on experience and instinct rather than science.

However, there had been substantial progress in understanding cereal chemistry.

An important innovation in the 1930s was the development and promotion of 'starch-reduced' bread. Reducing the proportion of starch in dough involved fortifying it with protein in the form of wet gluten, prepared at first by the baker himself and later sold commercially.

The technique for the recovery of wet gluten and starch from flour probably came to Australia from New Zealand early in the twentieth century and led in due course to the protein-enriched breads sold under licence as 'Procera' and 'Promax'. Higher protein content in flour produced dough with higher gluten content and, consequently, greater elasticity. The major advantages of this to the baker were improved handling, a wider margin for error through a more 'forgiving' dough, and, ultimately, better bread.[75]

Another important step towards a more scientific approach to baking was the 1947 decision to establish the Bread Research Institute of Australia Limited in New South Wales with the purpose of improving the quality of bread. The Institute later became BRI Australia Limited and then RoseWood Research. It was an independent national organisation committed to investing in ideas and research that was beneficial to the broader grain and grain product industry. It conducted research into the quality, milling and processing of grains, and was an independent centre of expertise in milling and baking.

A third significant development was the growth of Bread Manufacturers' Associations. First established in the late nineteenth century, these state and local associations gave master bakers a voice to government and employees' associations and became powerful and influential as the twentieth century progressed. In 1950, for example, the Queensland association decided to appoint a Research Officer.

Better Bread Standard To Be Sought
RESEARCH OFFICER MAY BE APPOINTED IN Q'LD.

BRISBANE, May 30.—The appointment of an overseas scientist as a research officer to improve Queensland bread standards has been recommended to the Queensland Bread Manufacturers' Association by its research sub-committee.

The man suggested, who was recommended by Sir Stanton Hicks, of the Adelaide University, is Mr. Alexander Brasch, who is aged 30, holds the diploma of inorganic chemistry of the University of Danzig, but is at present engaged in clerical duties at the migrants' hostel, Finsbury, South Australia. If he is selected the Department of Labour and National Service will arrange for his release.

Mr. T. B. Condie, in his presidential report to be presented to next week's meeting, states that he is convinced that scientific research in the bread industry will prove of untold value. Bread was the most important item in the community's diet, and should be of the best possible standard.

31 MAY 1950, P2. QUEENSLAND TIMES

The use of additives also began in the 1960s. Ascorbic acid (Vitamin C), for example, was widely used as an instant 'Bakerine'[p] and remained popular into the early 1970s, enabling small bakeries/hot bread shops to flourish because of the shorter fermentation time required.

But for all these advances, the equipment, techniques and fundamental process of making bread in the traditional bakehouse continued, virtually unchanged.

The process began at the mixer, a vital item of equipment in the mid-twentieth century bakehouse. Either one-armed or two-armed, a large mixer held sufficient dough for a standard four-bag batch which would produce 400 two-pound (0.9 kg) loaves. This meant the bowls were typically about 1.5 m in diameter, 0.75 m high, and were moved on castors.

The baker would lift the bags of flour, each weighing 150 lb (68 kg), up over the edge of the bowl and pour the flour in. Each batch required four bags of flour and bakeries had to produce several doughs each night to meet demand, especially at peak times such as Christmas and Easter. It was hard, physical work.

Even the empty flour bags had value. Some were used to cover benches or doughs during the bread-making process; some were fashioned into thick, double-layered 'oven mitts' with a slit on one side through which the baker inserted his hand; and the remainder were bundled into rolls (11 bags inside a twelfth bag) and returned to the flour mill for a credit.

Once the 600 lb (272 kg) of flour were in the bowl, the baker would apply the 'two per cent rule' and add 12 lb (5.5 kg) each of salt, fat and yeast, as well as water, and mix the dough for 30 minutes. The fat was added in chunks and because salt inhibits the action of yeast, great care had to be taken to keep it away from the yeast and not to oversalt the mix. It was also vital to ensure that the combined temperature of the dry mix and the water was at the critical level of 132°F (55.5°C). This was the temperature which would ensure that the fermentation time of every dough was predictable.

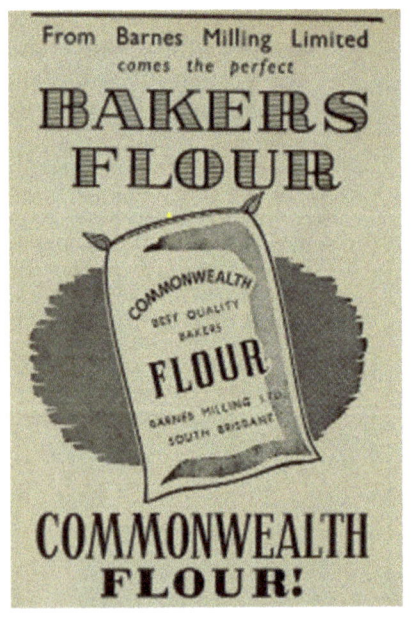

---

p   Bakerine was (and remains) a popular 'bread improver', an additive used to improve the texture/tenderness of the bread as well as its colour and taste.

As Michael Carter explains:

> First, the temperature of the flour in the bowl was taken, then the required temperature of the water was calculated by subtracting the flour temperature from 132°F. In hot weather, cooler water was required and vice versa in cold weather. At the bakeries where I worked in Warwick, we had both a refrigerated water supply and hot water. When my Dad operated his bakery in Esk, he had to buy ice in big blocks from the butter factory during very hot weather.

Added to these challenges was the yeast itself. Bakeries generally used compressed yeast, a soft, crumbly block of fresh yeast cells, beige in colour, which had to be kept refrigerated.

In addition to the challenge of refrigeration, there were problems of supply, exacerbated by occasional problems with batches of bread. In such circumstances, bakeries often borrowed yeast from each other. As Michael Carter recalls of his time at French's bakery in the early 1960s:

> If you lost a four-bag batch, there went 12 lb of yeast! If there was not enough for a replacement batch, bakeries would call each other and arrange for someone to pick up emergency yeast and drop back replacement supplies when their own delivery arrived. If the loss of a batch meant we couldn't meet a delivery deadline such as meeting a train, arrangements would even be made to 'borrow' bread from the opposition and replace it when our own was out of the oven.

Before Queensland's Department of Labour and Industry instigated the establishment of Compressed Yeast Co. (Queensland) Pty Ltd in Toowoomba in 1954, yeast supplies in Queensland had come from Sydney. The long distance and potential for dislocation of transport, combined with the highly perishable nature of yeast, meant that, in summer, yeast was not always readily available.

This meant that most early bakers and those in the first half of the twentieth century had their own recipes for potato yeast.

Some of those handwritten recipes have become family heirlooms.

NEW YEAST FACTORY

TOOWOOMBA—A compressed yeast factory which cost £250,000 to build was officially opened yesterday by the Transport Minister (Mr. Duggan).

Mr. Duggan said the new factory would employ 25 to 30 Toowoomba residents, would obtain its coal from Oakey, and use thousands of tons of flour milled from wheat grown on the Downs.

The factory will supply yeast to master bakers throughout the State.

FRI 1 OCT 1954. P6. CM

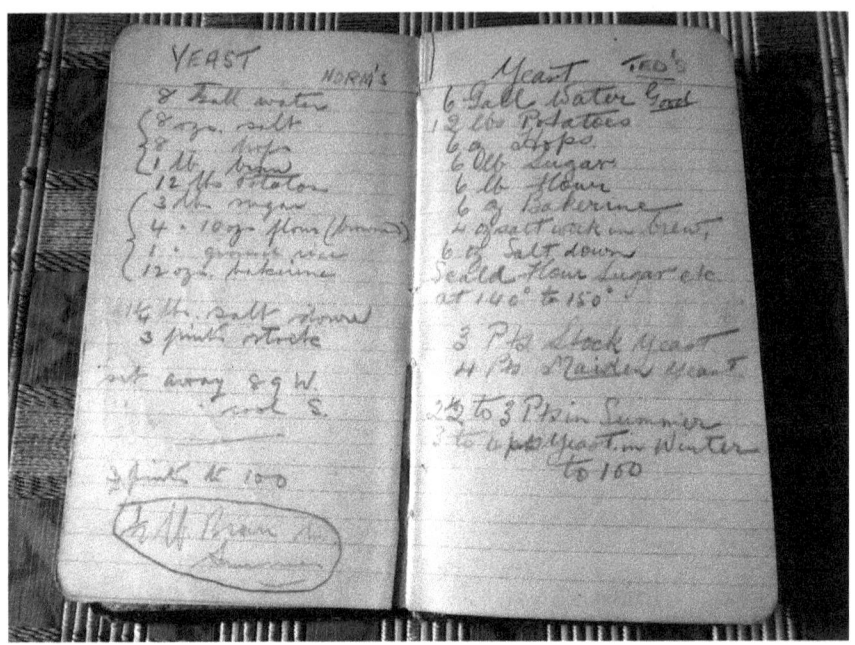

Fred Parker's recipes for yeast. (Author's photograph, September 2021.)

Fred Parker recorded his recipes for 'Norm's yeast' and 'Ted's yeast' in a pocket notebook which is now in the keeping of his son Ray ('Curley') Parker and his wife, Doreen. Similarly, the family of Neville McFarlane have his handwritten recipe for 'Bowe's Yeast', preserved from the time when he worked for Bowe's bakery in Pittsworth.

The next step in the dough-making process required the mixed dough to be covered and left to rise or 'ripen'. This sometimes involved adding extension rings to the bowl to allow space for the dough to rise.

After close to three hours, it was tested and, like so much in the baking process, the 'ripeness' test was largely intuitive and based on experience. The baker would simply push the four fingers of one hand into the dough up to the knuckles, pull them out and then just wait and observe. If the dough retained the indentation made by the fingers, it was ripe; any variation and it was either 'green' or 'over-ripe'. Ripe dough was then 'knocked' or 'punched' down in the bowl before being moved into sections of a trough.

For the next stage ('scaling off'), the bakers would drop each section of dough onto floured bags spread on top of the covered trough and cut it into the required loaf weights using a simple scraper blade and a mechanical weighing scale.

Each piece was weighed (2 lb 3 oz for a 2 lb loaf), moulded or 'rounded' and set aside to rest for 30 minutes. The speed and accuracy of this process was such that a batch of 400 loaves could be scaled off by a skilled tradesman in 30 minutes – less than five seconds per loaf.

In fact, scaling off had to be achieved in this time because doughs were mixed continuously. Once the first batch was in the mixer, the ingredients for the next batch were weighed and prepared so that, as each bowl was released from the mixer and wheeled away, covered, and left to rise, the waiting bowl of dry ingredients could be wheeled into place.

In the final stage, the rested, risen rounds were 'tinned-up'. Each piece was moulded either by machine or by hand into the required loaf shape. This was a precise and mechanically repetitious job – a full loaf required a two-hand method; a 'married' loaf, one hand for each half. After moulding, the loaves were placed in tins (or on trays for Vienna style loaves) and rested for a further 20 to 30 minutes, moistened, and covered (or sometimes placed in a steam room to hasten the process) before being ready for the oven.

Loading the oven was a two-man job with one baker placing the tins on the peel and the other positioning them in the oven. Loaves were typically baked for 30 minutes at the end of which they were removed from the oven, knocked out of the tins onto a bench, and set aside to cool.

Every oven had its hot and cold spots and individual quirks, and knowing those idiosyncrasies was the difference between success and a trip to the rubbish dump with a failed batch. Consequently, bakers knew their ovens intimately and, while ovens were often fitted with a pyrometer, a traditional baker sometimes preferred to cast a handful of flour into the oven to test the temperature – if the flour flared on contact with the hot air, it was ready.

Such hints of alchemy have always existed side by side with the science and art of baking.

Old bakers would squeeze a handful of flour to test its protein strength – the protein level was high if the flour retained its form; if it was weak, the form fell apart in the hand. They would also test the development of gluten in the dough by stretching out a small piece and holding it up to the light in a thin curtain. If the gluten is undeveloped, it shows as strings in the dough and needs more mixing. At the other extreme, too much mixing can overdevelop the gluten. The dough then begins to lose its elasticity, won't hold its shape when moulded, and won't rise properly in the tin or oven.

The description of the bread-making process above was supplied by Michael Carter.

A self-described 'bakery brat', Michael was born into the baking trade in 1950 as the son of William (Bill) Carter. Bill had done his apprenticeship at a bakery in Toogoolawah and, after Army service in WWII, worked for Dallymore's Bakery at Millmerran and re-opened a closed bakery in Esk in the 1950s. In 1962, he started work for Rex and Lyla French at French's Bakery at 32A King St, Warwick.

As Bill's son, Michael became a carter's assistant at French's Bakery at the end of the school year in 1963 and an apprentice in February the following year. He continued to work there in 1965 after the business was acquired by Jack and Trevor Sheeran and renamed Warwick Bakeries, and later when it became Regal Bakeries after being sold to Defiance Mills in the early 1970s.

In 1974, Michael and his wife Margaret opened Nanna's Hotbread and Cake Shop at 103 and later 129 Palmerin St. They sold their business to Joe Hall in 1980 and left Warwick in 1981, but Michael's interest in bread and baking continued into his later career in electronics as a Technician and Technical Officer for Telecom. In retirement, he remains a baker at heart and still enjoys turning his hand to making a dough from scratch by hand.

Frank Lawrence (L) and unidentified baker in the bakehouse at Brown's Bakery in the late 1930s. (Photograph from author's collection.)

STAYING OUT OF TROUBLE

Industrial action has been part of Australian history ever since 1791 when convicts went on strike for weekly rations.

However, it became much more common in the nineteenth century. Small workers' societies had emerged in the 1830s, but it was during the gold rushes of the 1850s that an active union movement first developed. Working class activists from around the world, including those who had been involved in the British labour movement and the struggle for Irish independence, became involved in demands for miners' rights on the gold fields, culminating in the Eureka Stockade in 1854.

Unions then flourished, among them the NSW Operative Bakers' Association, established in October 1869. The Association addressed a range of issues, particularly wage discrepancies between large and small bakeries, the requirement to work unlimited hours seven days a week, and the standard of accommodation provided to bakers on the premises, many of them being required to sleep on the top of the ovens.

Working long and inconvenient hours in hot, unpleasant conditions inevitably led to disputes between bakers and masters. Bakers' strikes in Queensland made the news in the *Warwick Argus* in both 1886 and 1891.

While employers and employees were often pitted against each other, both were subject to government-imposed regulations and limitations.

Brisbane.
[FROM OUR OWN CORRESPONDENT.]
February 21.

About thirty-five bakers went out on strike yesterday. Only seven of the employers have given way as yet, the others having taken a firm stand against the demands of the men. A meeting of journeymen bakers will be held to-morrow to discuss the situation.

TUE 23 FEB 1886. P2. WA.

STRIKE OF BAKERS. — The journeymen bakers of Brisbane struck work on Saturday morning. About forty men have gone out, and although the journeymen admit that the masters may be able to get men to fill their places, they contend that they will be able to harass the masters by bringing a strong boycott to bear upon them. This can be done by the working classes refusing to purchase bread from any baker who does not employ union hands.

TUE 17 MAR 1891. P2. WA

Release of 130 Bakers Sought

BRISBANE: A deputation from the Associated Bread Manufacturers' Association yesterday asked Mr Holloway, Minister for Labour, for the release of 130 operative bakers from the Services. They stated that bakers in many country towns were carrying on with little or no assistance, and some would have soon to close. At least 80 were required for the country, while 30 were required in Brisbane.

Mr Holloway undertook to make immediate representations to Mr Forde, and said he would instruct the local manpower officer to contact the military authorities in Brisbane to see what could be done.

FRI 15 DEC 1944. P1.

The impact of government restrictions was felt particularly strongly during World War II and led to collaboration among the master bakers in Warwick.

The Warwick Master Bakers' Association was formed to take action on issues of shared concern. One such instance was in 1941 when, owing to the wartime scarcity of paper, an advertisement was published, asking the public to 'bring their own wrapping paper when obtaining bread at the Association's bakery shops'.[76]

In October 1942, after consultation with the Department of War and Organisation of Industry, the Association became a limited liability company, the Warwick Bread Distributing Company, as a means of meeting the challenges of wartime petrol rations and shortages of tyres and manpower.[77] All household and country deliveries ceased at the end of that month with the six bread manufacturers pooling their output and delivering to shops and cafes where customers could purchase their bread. In a further move, only two carters were employed by the Company instead of the 16 who had worked for the six independent bakeries.

The Company became a vocal and influential group which was approached for its comments on everything from price rises and flour quality to the issues of Sunday baking, Saturday deliveries, and the 1944 bakers' strike in Townsville. The views of the Company were still being sought as late as December 1950.[78]

The Associated Bread Manufacturers' Association also became a powerful group.

The shortage of bakers towards the end of World War II prompted the Association to seek the urgent release of operative bakers from the armed services.[79] While 36 bakers were released from service in January 1945,[80] more than one master baker had resorted to supplying negative references for their staff during the War in an attempt to prevent their acceptance into the Armed Services.

One exceptionally creative example, preserved in the collection of one Warwick baking family, was written by Martin Brown of Brown's Bakery in May 1941:

> *I am firstly of the opinion that nothing but a one hundred per cent effort on our part will win this war and also that the RAAF is no place for duds.*
>
> *This young fellow has been with me for six years. By private arrangement with his parents, I have tried to teach him a trade but with very poor results as he has no initiative whatever and is totally unreliable. This may seem a hard thing to say but it is true as I know him better than his own mother. What is more, he has not an atom of courage.*
>
> *I am quite aware that you want all the men you can get and far be it from me to put any obstacle in your path but I am certain that this young fellow is not the type you are looking for.*

It appears that the Attesting Officer saw through the ruse because the cowardly, unreliable 'dud' with no initiative was promptly enlisted.

Both bakers and their masters were also under the constant scrutiny of industrial inspectors who were always on the lookout for breaches related to working hours and other regulations.

In addition, competing bakers kept a sharp eye on each other in relation to working hours because starting to bake earlier than one's competitors meant bread could be delivered earlier. Bakers did not hesitate to report any such instances of unfair competition.

The 1936 report in the *Warwick Daily News* on the next page is one example. In this case, three of the six master bakers then operating in Warwick were reported and fined. Similarly, more than one baker was fined in a 1937 case and, in 1947, two cases involving the same baker were reported within six months, each of them for starting work before the prescribed time of 5.00 am. However, as the 1947 report demonstrates, bakers were occasionally able to take advantage of loopholes in the regulations to avoid a fine.

MASTER BAKERS

FINED FOR AWARD BREACH

COMPLAINT LODGED IN BRISBANE

CARTING BEFORE TIME

During prosecutions against three bakery firms in the summons court yesterday, it was disclosed that such proceedings were the outcome of a complaint made to the authorities in Brisbane by a Warwick baker.

The defendants yesterday were Stanley Alex Munro Cain and Alfred Thorne, carrying on business as Cain and Thorne, Victor Emanuel Elsley, Harold Victor Elsley and Ellis Edward Elsley, carrying on business as V. Elsley and Sons, Norman Richings Tucker and Alfred Richings Tucker, carrying on business as Tucker Bros. The complaints were similar, Cain and Thorne being charged with committing a breach of the Bakers and Pastry Cook Carters' Award in that they permitted an employee, William Rosendahl, to cart before the fixed time of 6.30 a.m. on February 22. Proceedings against V. Elsley and Sons related to an employee named Leslie Bell, and against Tucker Brothers referred to an employee named Arthur Flitcroft.

The complaints in each instance were laid by the industrial inspector (Mr. W. Hunter).

TUE 24 MAR 1936. P2.

BAKERS FINED
Breach of Award.

In the Industrial Court yesterday, before Mr. W. P. Wilson, P.M., Martin Ralph Brown, baker, of Albion-street, and Alfred Thorne and Stanley Alex Munro Cain, trading as Cain and Thorne, Percy-street, were charged with having committed breaches of the bakers and pastrycooks' award, southern and Mackay division, Brown with having worked in his bakehouse at work other than dough making before the prescribed starting time of 7 a.m., and Cain and Thorne with having permitted an employee to work before the prescribed starting time. Defendants pleaded guilty.

Mr. W. M. Hunter, who prosecuted, said that this was the first offence and he therefore was not pressing for a heavy penalty.

A fine of £1, with 6/ costs of court, in default seven days, was inflicted in each case.

SAT 1 MAY 1937. P2.

Dismissed
Industrial Charge Against Baker

"Benefit of Doubt"

A complaint against Harold Gordon Clarke, a member of the firm of Clark and Glasby, bakers, of having committed a breach of the industrial award by doing bakers' work other than dough-making in his bakehouse before the prescribed starting time of 5 a.m. was dismissed by Mr H. B. Carney, SM, yesterday.

Mr Carney said that a doubt had been raised in his mind as to the nature of the dough, and he must give the defendant the benefit of that doubt.

The defence was that the dough in question was not for bread-making, but was being used in the manufacture of bun loaves, which came under the pastry-cooks' award. Defendant was represented by Mr T. H. Stabler.

The District Industrial Inspector (Mr D. Swain), who prosecuted, admitted that when he made his inspection on July 30 he had not had a close look at the dough in the trough at the bakehouse.

TUE 23 SEP 1947. P4.

The illuminated Certificate of Membership of the NSW Operative Bakers' Association is rich in detail – the two bakers in their caps and aprons proudly hold the tools of their trade (a peel and scuffle[q]); the three-word slogan of the Association (recreation, labour, rest) is illustrated by bucolic images and a beehive; a pattern of interlinked 8s represents the eight-hour day; solidarity is represented by the handshake and by the title 'Bro.' (Brother) before the certificate holder's name; and the illustration of the bakehouse shows each stage of the bread production process. (Image K3773, Noel Butlin Archives Centre, Australian National University.)

---

q   See p. 109.

WARWICK'S FLOUR MILLS

Despite the now infamous nineteenth century opinion[r] that the Darling Downs 'would not even grow cabbages', wheat farming was successful from the very early days of settlement.

However, flour was a different matter.

In the 1840s and 1850s, flour still had to be shipped to Brisbane from Sydney and South Australia through agents, as in the advertisement below for the flour of Sydney miller, Thomas Barker and Co., the first steam-powered mill in Australia.[81]

Fine Flour.

THE undersigned having been appointed SOLE AGENTS in Moreton Bay for the sale of Messrs. THOS. BARKER & CO.'S FLOUR, beg to inform the public in general, that they will always have a large stock on hand, which will be offered at Sydney prices, with the addition of freight only; the quality will be guaranteed.

Parties sending orders from the country may depend upon the best quality being forwarded.

J. & G. HARRIS.

North Brisbane, 20th Dec., 1858.

SAT 25 DEC 185. P3. MBC

---

r   Attributed to John Watts, the first parliamentary representative for Drayton, near Toowoomba (Cited by Adamson, T.J., in Wheat Growing and Milling, *Darling Downs 1840-1940*, p. 61)

In Warwick, the need for flour from southern sources changed when Charles Clark and James McKeachie established Warwick's first flour mill, Ellenthorpe (also recorded as Ellinthorp) Steam Flour Mill in 1861.

Charles George Henry Carr Clark[82] was a pastoralist and politician as well as a miller. Born into colonial gentry at Ellenthorpe Hall in what was then Van Diemen's Land in 1830, he gained valuable pastoral experience through his father on the family estate and would also have been aware of the milling trade because of the brief but profitable

Charles G.H.C. Clark. (Photograph courtesy State Library of Queensland.)

career of his father, G.C. Clark, as a miller. The milling business had enabled Clark Snr to build a grand two-storey stone home, Ellenthorpe Hall, near the Tasmanian town of Ross in 1826 using convict labour.

Charles moved to the Darling Downs in 1861 and immediately commenced business as a storekeeper in Warwick and as a miller in partnership with James

Ellenthorpe Mill. (Image sourced from French M. and Waterson D., *The Darling Downs – A Pictorial History,* p. 94.)

McKeachie.[s] The partners went on to make their mark on history as the first successful flour millers in Queensland.[83] Charles and his brother George, bought Old Talgai station in 1868 and, from 1871 to 1873, Charles represented Warwick in the Queensland Legislative Assembly. He died in Tenterfield in September 1896.

In 1874, the Ellenthorpe mill passed into the hands of Jacob Horwitz who was to run it for the next 12 years. The Agricultural Correspondent for *The Brisbane Courier* provided a very detailed description of the mill following a visit in 1876.[84]

Horwitz (also spelled Horowitz) was born in 1830 in East Prussia (part of Poland since World War II) and, together with his brother, came to Warwick where they ran a general store, the Exchange Store, before acquiring the mill in 1874. Horwitz also served as Mayor of Warwick from 1876 to 1878, resigning to contest the seat of Warwick in the Queensland Legislative Assembly. He was elected to the seat in 1878, and went on to serve two terms as member for the district until 1887. In February of that year, he travelled to Europe, submitting his resignation from parliament by cablegram from London, four months later. He was a prominent philanthropist on the Darling Downs, one of his most generous donations being 'a munificent gift' of £7,500[85] to the Warwick General Hospital in 1912 for the creation of a new ward.[86] He died in Berlin on 24 March 1920.

J. Horwitz and Co. Steam Flour Mill.
(Image sourced from Picture Queensland, State Library of Queensland.)

---

s   Both men are listed in the 1868 Warwick business directory alongside Gilm, the so-called 'German baker' in Fitzroy St, and James McDougall, the baker in Palmerin St.

In 1886, just prior to Horwitz's departure for Europe, he disposed of the mill to Francis Kates who was to earn the reputation of building more flour mills than any other person or company in Queensland.[†] After acquiring Horwitz's mill, Kates extended the building and installed new Hungarian roller machinery before selling it at auction to Barnes, Archibald and Co. just two years later, in 1888.

Barnes Archibald and Co. Ltd Steel Roller Mills.
(Image sourced from Picture Queensland, State Library of Queensland.)

The Barnes of Barnes, Archibald and Co. was George Powell Barnes (pictured right), one of Warwick's most prominent citizens. Born in Victoria in 1856, he was educated in Queensland, and had worked as a cashier in various regional stores before opening his own store in Warwick in 1878. By 1880, the young entrepreneur had formed Barnes and Co. Ltd, with his brother, Walter, and T.F. Merry of Toowoomba, in order to control businesses in Warwick, Allora, Yangan and Roma St in Brisbane, as well as the former Horwitz mill.

George Powell Barnes.
(Image sourced from Picture Queensland, State Library of Queensland.)

Both Barnes brothers entered politics. George was a Member of the Legislative Assembly for 27 years from 1908 to 1935 while Walter served in several roles, including that of State Treasurer. George was also an alderman of the Warwick Town Council for nine years and contributed to many industry and community groups in the city, notably the Methodist Church. In 1910-11, Barnes had his 'trade palace' built on the corner of Palmerin and King Sts. He died in Brisbane in December 1949, aged 93.[87]

---

† Properties which Kates owned or in which he had an interest included Dominion Mill in Toowoomba, Ipswich Flour Mills. Maranoa Flour Mill at Roma, and the Allora Mills.

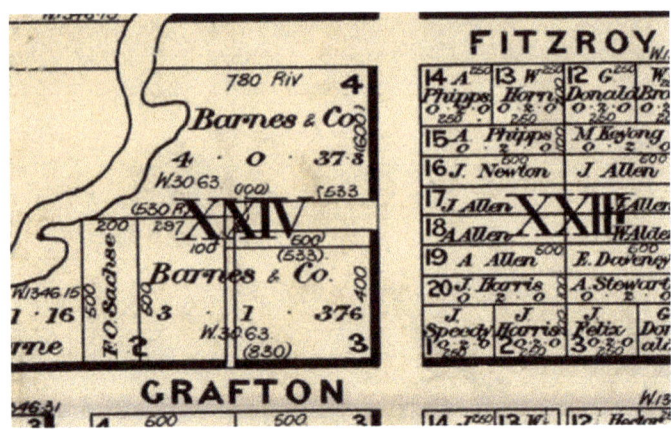

From plan of Warwick, 1879. (See Endnote 4.)

The map of late nineteenth century Warwick above shows the large footprint of the Barnes and Co. mill, extending from Wantley St to the banks of the Condamine, and spanning the block between Fitzroy and Grafton Sts. The contemporary map (p. 129) shows the same area in 2020, including Mill St, named in reference to the mill which once stood there.

In 1910, Barnes called tenders for the erection of a new, four-storey mill for his company in Lyons St. Following the destruction of the Mill Hill railway station by fire 1887, the East Warwick station in Lyons St was upgraded and the Barnes and Co. mill was one of many new industrial buildings and storage facilities erected from 1897 to take advantage of this.[88]

After 50 years of producing flour for Clark, Horowitz, Kates, and Barnes, most of the original 1861 mill in Wantley St was demolished when the Lyons St mill was constructed. The exception was the brick building which was acquired by Donald J. Hutchings, an English contractor and builder who worked in Warwick from 1911 until he enlisted in the AIF in September 1916. Hutchings sold the building to the Warwick Benevolent Society in 1915 and was then contracted by the Society to remodel it into a single-storey home for aged and infirm women. When completed, its facilities included 10 bedrooms, a kitchen, two bathrooms and a large lounge/dining room with a fireplace. The home was officially opened in October 1915 but following concerns of negative public perception of the term 'benevolent home', the Society renamed the building The Mill House in 1917.

It ceased operation as a nursing home in the mid-20th century after which the building remained vacant and neglected until the mid-1970s when it was acquired by Mrs Elaine Rogers, a widow with eight children. Some of the internal walls were removed at this time to create an eight-bedroom house.

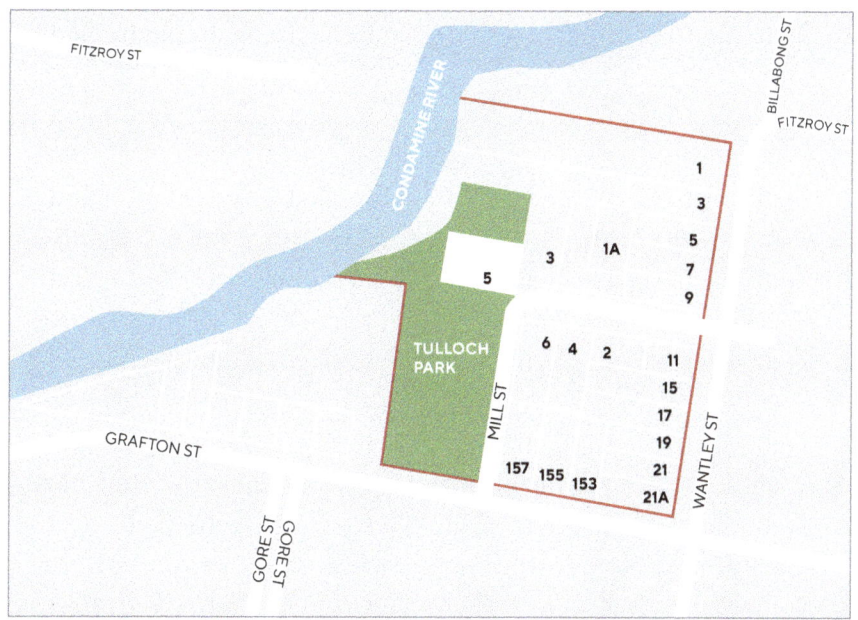

Street map of Warwick, 2021 showing previous location of Barnes and Co. mill.

The Mill House in Mill St, Warwick. (Author's photograph, September 2020.)

The house still includes many features of the 1915 renovations including numbers on each of the bedrooms and decorative ventilation panels. (Image courtesy of Maureen Kathage.)

The Mill House has remained a private home ever since, with the original room numbers and vents retained above the doors in the long central hallway.

The mill in Lyons St continued to operate as Barnes and Co. until 1938 when it was purchased by Simpson Bros. It remained in their control until 1951 when it was sold to Barnes' Commonwealth Milling Co.

The 1976 review of a merger case involving Barnes Commonwealth Milling Co. noted that the Brisbane company had once been one of the largest flour-millers in Queensland but, by the date of the merger case, was the smallest of the five still operating in the State. The review also noted that the company had owned a mill in Warwick 'ten years ago' (i.e. 1966) but that it had 'closed in the intervening period'.[89]

The precise date when the Lyons St mill ceased operation was not known at the time of writing, but closure, combined with a fire in the early 1970s, meant that by the mid-1970s, the building was stripped out to a shell with no floors and only the framing left. In a post on the *Lost Faces of Warwick and District* Facebook page, Roger Cox recalled: 'It sat for years – a four storey pigeon coop – until it had to come down before it fell down'.[90] Other posts on the same

Warwick Railway Station showing Barnes and Co. flour mill in Lyons St (c. 1912). (Image sourced from Picture Queensland, State Library of Queensland.)

Simpson Bros flour mill in Lyons St.
(Photograph courtesy of Dianne Crowe.)

Simpson's Mill Sold To Brisbane Firm

Messrs. Simpson Bros.' flour milling business in Lyon Street has been purchased by a Brisbane firm, Barnes' Commonwealth Milling Co. for an undisclosed figure.

In an exclusive statement yesterday, the manager of Barnes Commonwealth Milling Co. (Mr. W. Armstrong) said that, although he was unable to divulge more detailed information regarding the sale, the present method of operation of the mill would be unchanged.

The mill was purchased by Simpson Bros. in October, 1938, from Barnes and Co., Warwick, for a sum believed to be in the vicinity of £20,000.

This is the second important flour mill sale in Warwick in the last three months. In November last, Bunge Co. Ltd. (Australia) purchased the Mill Hill mill from the Warwick Co-operative Farmers' Milling Association for £55,000.

SAT 27 JAN 1951. P2.

BARNES' MILL

Purchase By Simpson Bros.

Price In Vicinity Of £20,000

Messrs. Simpson Bros. Proprietary, Ltd., of Brisbane, flour millers, have purchased the Warwick flour mill of Barnes and Co. Proprietary, Ltd. It is understood that the price paid is in the vicinity of £20,000. The South Brisbane mill of Messrs. Barnes and Co. was not involved in the sale.

Mr. G. P. Barnes, former member of Parliament for Warwick for many years, who is now in Brisbane, said last night that the mill was built by Mr. Charles Clarke, who sold it to Mr. Francis Kates, one time member for Cunningham. It was purchased by Barnes, Archibald and Company in 1888. Mr. Archibald retired from the firm later, and it was carried on by Barnes and Co. ever since.

Speaking for the purchasers last night Mr. E. P. Simpson said that the mill at present was working only one shift. It was hoped as soon as sufficient Queensland wheat was available to work three shifts a day. This would probably be in January next. The bulk of the output would be used for the manufacture of self-raising flour for the Simpson Bros. firm.

Mr. G. P. Barnes, founder of the firm of Barnes and Co., was born in Melbourne in 1856 and established the Warwick firm in 1878. There he was joined by his brother, Mr. W. H. Barnes, who became State Treasurer of Queensland, and the business, which included general stores as well as mills, extended to other Queensland towns and to the capital.

WED 5 OCT 1938. P4.

Facebook page record that some of the bricks and large pine floor joists were salvaged before it was finally demolished, together with the silos and ground storage for grain, leaving just part of one building which, in 2020, was the premises of Ray Bunch Machinery. Built from local sandstone, the remaining building has been designated by the Southern Downs Regional Council as having State significance because its role in Warwick's history.

Derelict Barnes' Mill, Lyons St, before demolition. (Photograph courtesy of Pamela Fisher.)

Remaining mill building, Lyons St. (Image capture: March 2010 © Google Australia.)

By 1873, growers' dissatisfaction with Clark and McKeachie at Ellenthorpe led to moves to establish a second flour mill in Warwick.

In February that year, a meeting of wheat farmers decided 'with considerable spirit and great earnestness of purpose'[91] to establish a co-operative and build their own mill. The Darling Downs Farmers' Co-operative Association was the result, with officers elected, rules agreed and the first shares issued at the second meeting of the Association on 12 March 1873.

Despite initial confidence that the mill would be gristing[u] wheat later that year, newspaper reports and the robust exchange of views conducted through Letters to the Editor of the town's two newspapers show that progress was slow, due principally to the challenge of raising the required capital.

Despite the public and farmers being urged to 'put their shoulders to the wheel', by the end of 1875, the mill was no nearer to completion. On 18 December that year the Warwick Correspondent for *The Queenslander* bitingly commented: 'The building now stands in a semi-state of completion – truly symbolical of the fate of all similar undertakings in Warwick'.

Confronted by insolvency, the Association was forced to abandon the building. However, the ever-entrepreneurial Francis Kates (p. 127), seizing another opportunity, purchased the mill in 1876, selling it almost immediately (and profitably) to New England brothers, William and Charles Hayes.

Original Correspondence.

[*We do not necessarily hold ourselves responsible for the opinions expressed by our correspondents.*]

CO-OPERATIVE FLOUR MILL.

(To the Editor of the Examiner and Times.)

Sir,—It is a difficult task to add to, or strengthen, the arguments recently used by different writers in both newspapers of this town urging the public in general, and the farmers in particular, to put their shoulders to the wheel of this enterprise, and not disgrace themselves by allowing it to pass into the hands of monopolists.

Monopoly in flour is a public curse, and particularly oppressive to the poor and helpless. There is a duty as well as interest, connected with good citizenship, to make a little sacrifice, to "cast bread upon the waters" for the public good. In hopes of success.

Yours, &c.,
A SHAREHOLDER.

SAT 22 AUG 1874. P2. WET

The Hayes brothers completed the mill, and gristing of the 1877 wheat harvest started on 3 December 1877.

The newly named Queensland Flour Mill was enthusiastically welcomed. On 13 December 1877, *The Warwick Argus and Tenterfield Chronicle* published a laudatory Letter to the Editor from a writer identifying himself only as 'One of Yourselves'. The quote on the following page is only a quarter of the total of 560 words.

---

u   Gristing is the process by which the miller blends various types of wheat in different proportions to produce different types of flour.

A few months ago, the Farmers' Flour Mill was the laughing stock of the whole colony. This wide-spread ridicule was well earned by the idiotic conduct of many of the farmers themselves, but by the greatest good fortune, the mill has at last fallen into the hands of men who know thoroughly what they are about. The Messrs Hayes appear determined to give wheat growers in this district what they certainly never got before, that is, fair play, fair value, and gentlemanly civility. Of course, you all remember your past treatment – half-price, preposterously long-dated bills, and vulgar, boorish insolence. The advent of Messrs Hayes has for the first time shattered the bondage under which you have hitherto been crushed.... Had I ten thousand bushels they should have every ounce of it.

The Hayes brothers changed the name to Queensland Steam Roller Mills and continued to operate it until 1891.

The reputation enjoyed by the Hayes brothers seems to have driven competitors to extraordinary lengths. In March 1882, the cautionary advertisement (right) appeared in the *Warwick Argus* and, three years later, in a 'back to the future' move, a co-operative milling enterprise was again mooted.

> **CAUTION.**
>
> As we are in possession of reliable information that FLOUR OF INFERIOR MAKE is being put into our bags and sold as OUR FLOUR; We hereby give notice that if this practice is continued we shall be compelled to take such steps as will effectually stop it.
>
> W. & C. HAYES,
> 208   Queensland Flour Mills.

TUE 7 MAR 1882. P3. WA

A detailed prospectus for the Warwick Farmers' Cooperative Milling Association, was published in the *Warwick Daily News* on 31 January 1885 and by November 1890, capital of £50,000 had been raised, enabling the Association to register the Warwick Farmers' Milling Co. Ltd. The following month, Charles Hayes and Co. sold the mill to the new company. The company continued to operate the mill until a fire in 1943 after which it remained dormant until c. 1950[92] when it was purchased by Bunge (Australia) Pty Ltd, trading then as Warwick Flour Mills. Bunge rebuilt the mill (retaining one of the original sandstone walls) and continued to operate it until c. 1970 when it closed as a flour mill, leaving only the stock feed section until that, too, closed.

Warwick was a microcosm of the flour milling and bread manufacturing industry in Australia at this time. It was a period of great change, much of which was due to the establishment of English-based company, George Weston Foods, in Australia. This brought about greater competition for flour sales and the development of pre-mixed products for bakeries. This was also the era that saw the development of supermarkets, large-scale commercial bakeries and extensive transport networks, all of which had an impact.

Hayes' Queensland Steam Flour Mills c. 1885 before its sale to Warwick Farmers' Milling Co. (Image sourced from Picture Queensland, State Library of Queensland.)

Warwick Farmers' Milling Co. mill, 1904. (Photograph by M.H. Poulson from *The Queenslander*. Courtesy of State Library of Queensland.)

However, the mill on Churchill Drive had by no means reached the end of its life. After surviving more than a century of different owners as well as fire, flood, World Wars, economic depressions and the volatility of the grain market, it entered yet another stage in its history in 1989 when it was sold to Toowoomba company, Defiance and recommissioned as a special-purpose maize milling plant.

Defiance itself was well named. The founder, Ellen O'Brien, was a mother of 10 who took over management of the Toowoomba milling business when her husband died in 1906 and oversaw its expansion until her death in 1924. Fittingly, she was inducted into the Queensland Business Leaders Hall of Fame in 2015 and the brand she built remains on Australian supermarket shelves.

By the mid-1990s, Defiance had developed a substantial international profile, exporting its products to markets including Japan, Korea, Thailand and New Guinea.

In c. 1998, it was sold to Goodman Fielder, but because this company also operated the Allied Milling Company, this meant that the only two maize mills in Australia would be controlled by a single company. Faced by objections from the Australian Competition and Consumer Commission (ACCC), Goodman Fielder sold the Warwick maize mill to Bunge Industrial.

In 2003, the New Zealand company, Corson Grain Ltd, acquired the mill to produce a wide range of maize products. In 2020, the mill was the sole supplier of 'flaking grits' to Kellogg's Australia for the production of Kellogg's® Corn Flakes.

Calico flour bags from the Warwick Farmers Co-operative Milling Association Ltd and its successor, Warwick Flour Mills. (Photographs courtesy of Rod Campbell.)

WARWICK'S BAKEHOUSES

The traditional, wood- and gas-fired bakeries in the era covered by this history had brick ovens and a large footprint.

Apart from the bakehouse and the 'Scotch' ovens (see p. 101), they needed garaging for carts and, later, for motorised vehicles. They also needed a paddock for the cart horses and storage for flour, firewood, and saddlery, as well as chaff and oats for the horses. Many also had accommodation attached because bakers needed to begin making doughs late at night or in the very early hours of the morning.

Details have been found of seven bakeries of this kind in Warwick.

At the time of writing, none of the bakehouses themselves remained, but five associated buildings were still standing – the Bochman Buildings in Grafton St, Derby House at 149 Palmerin St, the bakery shop at 58 Grafton St, Elsleys at 148 Palmerin St, and Cain and Thorne's shop on the corner of Percy and Palmerin Sts.[v] The Bochman Buildings and Derby House are protected by local heritage legislation.[93]

The successive owners/occupants of each site are listed where known.

---

v   While the street numbers of Derby House and Elsleys are consecutive, the buildings are on opposite sides of Palmerin St and in different city blocks.

32A King Street

SUCCESSION

1914 .... Henry Tucker

1951.................. Mervyn Willett

c. 1960 .... Rex and Lyla French

1970s .... Trevor and Margaret Sheeran

Mid-1970s........ ceased operating as a bakery

King St was not included in the original Warwick town plan but in 1907, local businessman, George Powell Barnes (see p. 127), offered the Warwick Town Council the land from Palmerin St to Lyons St as a gift for the construction of a new street.

The offer was driven primarily by commercial rather than civic motives, as Barnes wanted to establish a new department store in Palmerin St with dual frontages. Since the disastrous floods of 1887 and 1893, he had seen the town expanding to the south and west, away from the Condamine River, and wanted to take advantage of this. Once the contract was signed in 1910, the Barnes Building was constructed on the corner of Palmerin and King Sts and other businesses quickly sprang up along the new street.

Among them was the bakery which Henry Tucker acquired at 32A King St in 1914. Details of the Tucker family ownership to 1951 are in the section on Henry Tucker and the Tucker Brothers (p. 86).

The bakery was sold in May 1951 to pastrycook Mervyn G. Willett and his wife, Joan M. Willett, and was next acquired by Rex and Lyla French in the early 1960s when the Willetts relocated to the premises on the corner of Palmerin and Fitzroy Sts. Willetts Cake Shop remained there until 1968 when the business was purchased by Owen and Margaret Mollenhauer, trading as Mollies (short for Mollenhauer) Cake Shop.

Tucker's Hygienic Bakery (later Tucker and Sons and Tucker Bros.) in the 1930s. All three trading names from its first 50 years life as a bakery can be seen. (Photograph from author's collection.)

After the Frenches left Warwick in 1964, the King St business was acquired by Jack Sheeran, a highly successful baker entrepreneur whose business model was to purchase bakeries, build them up and re-sell them. Over his life in business, Jack was to implement this strategy very successfully in many locations in NSW and Queensland — Nowra, Bowral, Coomera, Gympie, and the Brisbane suburbs of Norman Park and Taringa. Under Jack's ownership, the Taringa bakery became the most successful privately owned bread manufacturing business on the eastern seaboard, enabling him to sell it to Tip Top bakeries. Jack also made an enormous contribution to the Queensland Bread Manufacturers' Association, serving as President for 30 years and working tirelessly as an advocate for small, independent bakeries. The Jack Sheeran Churchill Fellowship was established in his name to advance the industry, particularly in Queensland, and supported the projects of eight Fellows between 1990 and 2006.

The bakery in King St was operated by Trevor Sheeran who had not entered the baking trade until the age of 40, but was to become an award-

32A King St, October 2020. (Photograph courtesy of Eric Turner.)

Access to the rear of the bakery at 32 King St was from Stewart Avenue, via a laneway behind the corner block (36 King St). The location of Derby House at 149 Palmerin St (p. 141) is also marked.

winning baker and pastrycook. Trevor and his wife Margaret ran the bakery in the early 1970s until, owing to increasing competition from Toowoomba Family Choice Bakery (owned by Defiance Milling), the business was sold to Defiance and it became Regal Bakery.

From this time, bread was manufactured in Toowoomba at the Family Choice Bakery, packaged as Regal Bread, and transported to the Regal Bakery in King St. Bread rolls, buns and other small lines were manufactured by Regal in Warwick and transported back to Toowoomba to be packaged under the Family Choice brand.

When the bakery was finally closed in the mid-1970s, it became, in turn, a second-hand shop operated by Mrs Bulmer and an informal amusement centre with pool tables, etc., operated by Mrs Creed. Following a fire, the building was demolished but a trace of the past life of the site remains in a section of tiled flooring in one of the current buildings. In late 2020 the site was owned and used by a nearby King St business, Warwick Automatic Transmission Service.

149 Palmerin Street (Derby House)

SUCCESSION

1935.................... Les Overstead and Cyril Tucker

1950.................... Fred Tanna

Details of the establishment and ownership of this bakery from 1935 are in the earlier sections on the Tuckers (p. 86) and the Oversteads (p. 73).

Since its construction in 1935, Derby House had included several shops in addition to the outlet for the bakery business (Warwick Bakery) operated by Cyril Tucker and Les Overstead.

Among the enterprises that prospered in this location was the fruit and vegetable shop of the Tanna family. The Tannas had settled in Toowoomba when they immigrated from Lebanon in 1926 but moved to Warwick in 1939, establishing their business the following year.[94] By December 1948, the business had grown to the extent that a shipment of 3,500 watermelons was ordered from Bowen, warranting a front-page photograph in the *Warwick Daily News*.[95]

In January 1950, Fred Tanna purchased the adjacent business, Warwick Bakery, from Cyril Tucker. He retained the business name but quickly expanded the range of products from the original bread, buns and rolls to a wide variety of pastries and cakes (including Christmas cakes) and sliced bread.

UNDER NEW MANAGEMENT
WARWICK BAKERY
TANNA'S
wish to advise they have Purchased WARWICK BAKERY BUSINESS in PALMERIN STREET.

Tanna's assure all Customers the same Business Arrangements that were in use shall be maintained

Experienced Bakers are at your service, and it will be pointed out these turn out the same High Class Bread that has always pleased Warwick Bakery Customers. The Popular PROMAX LOAVES, CURRANT and CINNAMON LOAVES, DOLLY VARDENS and BUNS are available at

WARWICK BAKERY
To save disappointment RING 440 and TANNA'S will keep your Order for you.

TUE 10 JAN 1950. P2.

WARWICK BAKERY SPECIALS
HOT CROSS BUN TIME
is back again, and Orders are being taken. All Orders are requested to be in by WEDNESDAY, APRIL 5.

The High Class of BREAD Manufactured by the WARWICK BAKERY is indicated by the fact that the WARWICK BAKERY out of 400 Entries in the recent Toowoomba Show gained 2nd Honours in BROWN BREAD and 3rd Prize in PROMAX.

SPECIAL! BREAD ROLLS! Ideal for all Social Events, are manufactured to suit your taste.

REMEMBER! If it's QUALITY you are looking for
WARWICK BAKERY
has QUALITY. RING 440 for YOUR ORDER.

THU 30 MAR 1950. P8.

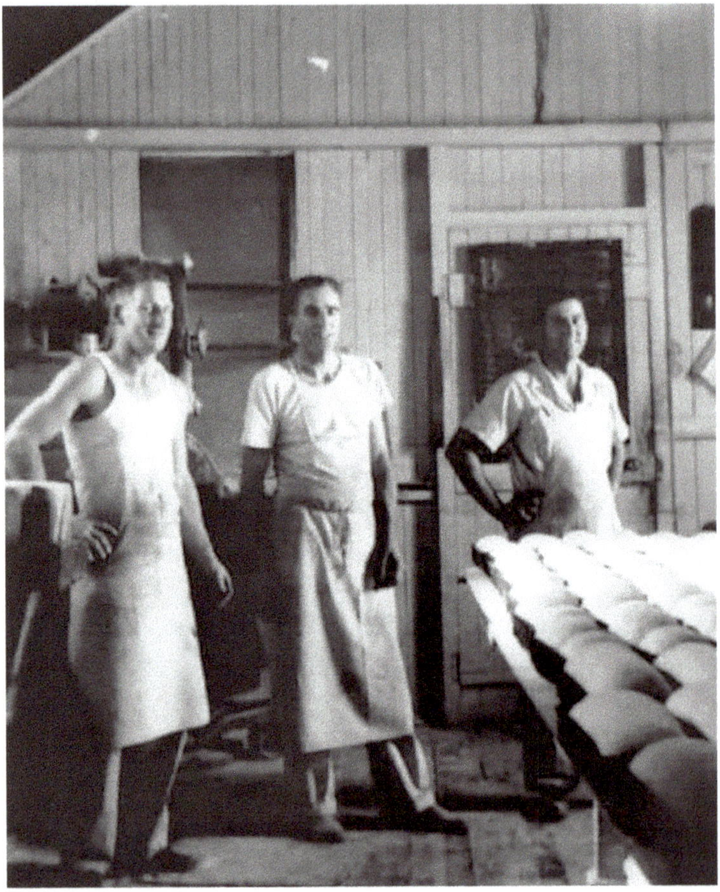

Mick Buggie, Frank Lawrence and Fred Tanna (L to R) in the bakehouse at Tanna's Bakery, date unknown. (Photograph courtesy of Peter Tanna.)

The grave of Fred and Jean Tanna, Warwick cemetery. (Photograph courtesy of Eric Turner.)

Shortly before she died in 2020 at the age of 86, the wife of Roger Schmidt (one of several bakers with links to Warwick Bakery) still clearly remembered the gold sheaf of wheat and red print which featured in the design of the waxed wrapping on their sliced bread.

Peter Tanna recalls that Gordon Clarke of Clarke and Glasby coined the name 'Pneumonia Lane' for the narrow passageway between Derby House and the adjacent building on its southern side – a very cold and draughty place in a Warwick winter. Peter also recalled Fred Tanna saying that the oven at 149 Palmerin St was 'the biggest and best in town'.

The Tannas continued to operate their business from the Palmerin St location, extending it to include a milk bar which, in 2018, was ranked No. 6 on the list of experiences that define a Warwick local: 'Having a malted milk and toasted ham-and-cheese sandwich at Tanna's milk bar'. In addition to earning fame through the fruit shop, bakery and milk bar, the Tannas were well known and respected in sport and entertainment circles. This led to yet another definition of a 'local': 'Anyone who has been a to a dance and hasn't heard Peter Tanna sing couldn't call themselves a long-term local'.[96]

The Tanna family left Warwick in 2004 except for matriarch, Jean Margaret, who died there in 2006, ending the family's 67-year association with the city. She is buried in Warwick Cemetery beside her husband, Frederick Joseph.

In 2020, Derby House was owned by Matthew Collins and offered retail space at street level and four large flats as rental accommodation upstairs.

'Pneumonia Lane' still separates Derby House from the adjacent building. (Author's photograph, February 2021.)

SOMETHING NEW
at
WARWICK BAKERY

TANNA'S Proprietors of WARWICK BAKERY have Obtained the Services of an EX-CELLENT **PASTRY-COOK** WITHIN THE NEXT FEW DAYS

Cakes and Pastry

WILL BE ON DISPLAY IN WARWICK BAKERY WINDOWS

Watch Out for Your Favourites.

WARWICK BAKERY HAVE EXCELLED IN THE PRODUCTION OF

* Buns
* Dolly Vardens
* Promax Rolls and
* Cinnamons

Now be Ready to Try Their CAKES!

SATISFACTION ASSURED.

REMEMBER! Buy the BEST. Forget the REST.

THE BEST IS ALWAYS AVAILABLE AT

Warwick Bakery

TUE 14 NOV 1950. P6.

CAKES
at
WARWICK BAKERY

TANNA'S Proprietors of Warwick Bakery, wish to announce they now have the long promised Cakes —and a fine selection they are.

The Quality Speaks for itself. Already

* CHECKER BARS
* FRUIT BARS
* CHERRY BARS
* APPLE SLICES
* SULTANA BLOCK CAKE
* RAINBOW CAKE and
* CHOCOLATE CAKE

are becoming popular.

XMAS CAKES

Warwick Bakery have a Fine Cake on Display Now.

ORDERS MUST BE IN EARLY. ANY SIZE DESIRED WILL BE MADE.

See the High Quality of Cakes at

Warwick Bakery

WHERE ONLY THE BEST IS AVAILABLE.

WED 29 NOV 1950. P10.

41 Albion Street

SUCCESSION

1864 to 1888	possibly Benjamin Ingham and C.G. Clarkeo
1888	The Co-operative Baking Company
1894	C.G. Downs
1897	Louis Overstead
1898/9	Daniel Maunsell
1908	Henry Reading
1910	James Callaghan
1919	William Benner Blackburn
1920	Alexander Herbert Ross
1923	Mrs Pavey
1924	Mr Brown
1928	Frederick Parker
1931	Percy St Henry
1933	Martin Ralph Brown
1951	Ralph Ashley Brown
1966	Joseph and Mary Hall
2000	demolished

Albion St in the second half of the 19th century was Warwick's main thoroughfare with key buildings such as the Post and Telegraph Office located there.

While the early provenance of the bakehouse and eclectic collection of buildings which once stood at this site is not clear, Benjamin Ingham, C.G. Clarkeo, the Co-operative Baking Company, Charles G. Downs (also spelled Downes), Louis Overstead and Daniel Maunsell all advertised their businesses as operating in Albion St.

As no reference has been found to other bakeries in Albion St, and as several refer to their businesses as being 'opposite the Post and Telegraph Office' or 'next to Queen's Hotel', it seems likely that 41 Albion St was the location of all of these businesses. The 'confectioner' signage seen on the building at this location in the photograph taken during the 1887 flood (p. 22) is further evidence, and suggests that this was the site of one of Warwick's oldest bakeries.

It is known that Henry Reading operated the bakery in 1908. Two years later, in September 1910, he sold the bakery to James Callaghan and James Lowe and, together with his wife, Mary Jane, and two children, moved to the nearby village of Pratten to establish a bakery there.

Callaghan, meanwhile, operated the Albion St bakery for nine years until he sold it to William Benner Blackburn in March 1919.

Blackburn was an English baker who had come to Australia as an 18-year-old c. 1890, moving from NSW to Toowoomba c. 1906 and establishing his own bakery in Crows Nest. In addition to the business in Albion St, he operated a bakery in Tannymorel, retiring from the trade c. 1927 and purchasing 'Merino Park', a grazing property near Thane, where he died in April 1943.[97]

It is not known if the 'Spot Cash' bakery advertised on 6 December 1919 (p. 147) was Blackburn's business, but an advertisement less than three weeks later (p. 147) makes it clear that his tenure in Albion St was brief, as ownership of the bakery by then had transferred to Alexander Herbert Ross.

Cheap Bread ! Cheap Bread !
C. G. DOWNS

BEGS to inform the public of Warwick and surrounding district that he has taken the Premises in Albion-street, known as the "NATIONAL BAKERY," where he is NOW prepared to SUPPLY First-class BREAD at 2½d. per 2lb. Loaf. All kinds of Cakes and Confectionery always on hand. Balls, Picnics, and Wedding Parties catered for on the most reasonable terms. Patronise the man who works with the times. 579

SAT 12 JUL 1894. P2. WA

Public Notice

I, HENRY READING, have this day SOLD my BUSINESS of BAKER in Warwick and District to Messrs. CALLAGHAN & LOWE. All DEBTS due to me must be PAID to Mr. C. RICHARDSON, Palmerin-st. (whose receipt will be sufficient discharge), on or before the 7th OCTOBER NEXT.

H. READING.
Warwick, September 20, 1910.

We, the undersigned, hereby wish to notify the public of Warwick and District that we have PURCHASED the above business, and trust, by strict attention to business and courtesy to customers, to merit a continuance of the support accorded to our predecessor. The business will be taken over by us from 1st October, from which date the price of bread will be 3½d. booked or 3d. cash (weekly accounts considered as cash).

J. CALLAGHAN.
JAS. LOWE.

SAT 24 SEP 1910. P5. WET

IMPORTANT SALES.

Messrs. Murphy & Parker report the sale, on account of Mr. Jas. Callaghan, of his bakery business in Albion-street, to Mr. Blackburn, of Toowoomba; also, on account of the executors of late John Sheahan, the lease, license and goodwill of the Stanthorpe Hotel, to Mr. John J. V. Walsh, of Emu Vale.

SAT 8 MAR 1919. P8.

> **WANTED** Known,—Best Bread now on Sale: 5d. at the shop, at Spot Cash Bakery, Albion-street (late Callaghan's); also at Jones and Brooks', King-street. 271

SAT 6 DEC 1919. P8.

> **ALEX. ROSS,**
> **WISHES** to notify the Residents of Warwick and District that he has commenced business as a BAKER in ALBION-STREET.
> **ALEX. ROSS,**
> BAKER, ALBION-STREET.

WED 24 DEC 1919. P8.

Ross, too, did not continue in business for long. In January 1923, he announced that he had sold the business to a Mrs Pavey, but her time in Albion St was even shorter than Blackburn's – in August, her household goods were auctioned because she was 'leaving Warwick'.

> **PUBLIC NOTICE.**
> HAVING disposed of my bakery business to Mrs. M. Pavey, I wish to thank my numerous customers for the support accorded me in the past, and solicit a continuance of same for Mrs. Pavey.
> All accounts owing to me must be settled before the end of the month to avoid proceedings for collection.
> **ALEX ROSS,**
> Albion Street, January 17. 545

FRI 19 JAN 1923. P1.

> **SALE BY PUBLIC AUCTION**
> OF Practically New SILKY OAK FURNITURE and HOUSEHOLD EFFECTS, Linoleum, &c., on account of MRS. M. PAVEY, Albion-street, who is leaving Warwick.
> Full particulars future issue.
> **V. W. RANSOME,**
> AUCTIONEER.

SAT 4 AUG 1923. P1.

The next owner appears to have been a Mr Brown (no relation of the Brown family on p. 51) because he is referred to in the advertisement below in January 1924 and the Queen's Hotel was on the corner of Fitzroy and Albion Sts, adjacent to the bakery.

> **FRIDAY NEXT, AT 2.30.**
> At Mr. Brown's Bakery, Albion-street (near Queen's Hotel), on account of Mr. Arthur Harf, who is leaving Warwick,

THU 17 JAN 1924.

The trail becomes clear in 1927 when Fred Parker left the bootmaking trade and set up business there as a baker. Four years later, on 1 July 1931, he sold the bakery to Percy St Henry for £850.00. St Henry, in turn, sold the business to Martin Brown in April 1933.

For the next 33 years, the bakery remained in the hands of the Brown family, first Martin and then, from 1951, his son Ralph. In 1966, Ralph sold the business to Joe and Mary Hall. When the Halls left Warwick, the bakery ceased to operate and was demolished c. 2000 as part of site preparation for the construction of an Aldi supermarket and carpark.

Amy Brown in the bakery yard beside one of the WWII Blitz buggies restored by Ralph Brown for use at Brown's Bakery to cart wood, flour, etc. The sheds in the background were used to garage delivery carts and the small shed on the right was used for flour storage. It housed a resident python to keep mice at bay. (Photograph from author's collection, c. 1944.)

Amy and Judith Brown in the lane beside the bakehouse c. 1947 with the Brown family home at 39 Albion St under construction in the background and the Army tent used by the family as accommodation while the house was under construction. The house has since been removed and in 2021 the site is occupied by the Warwick office of Centrelink. (Photograph from author's collection.)

The bakery was a complex of single-storey buildings accessed from Albion St by a laneway which emerged in Fitzroy St. The building fronting Albion St was divided into two flats which served as accommodation for bakers. Originally, the awning shaded a shop-front but this was not used as a shop at least from 1933. (Author's photograph, 1998.)

The flats fronting Albion St were accessed via a gate beside a shed which housed both a laundry for the occupants of the flat and a small room in which the pastrycook worked. The reinforced brick and stone wall was the side of the bakehouse. (Author's photograph, 1998.)

148 Palmerin Street (Elsleys)

SUCCESSION

1918.................Godfrey Bernard McInnes

1923.................Cecil Smith Ward

1934.................Edward Mulhall

1935.................Victor Elsley

1937.................Herbert George Glasby

1938.................Frederick Parker

1976.................ceased operating as a bakery

Although there are hints of earlier bakeries on this site, the first owner for which there is a definitive record is Godfrey Bernard McInnes who advertised in 1918 that he had 'removed from Grafton-street'[98] to more commodious and better-appointed premises situated in Palmerin-street and near to Wood-street'.[99]

A week before announcing his 'removal', a barely disguised advertorial was published for the Allen's Patent Steel Oven which McInnes had installed at the new bakery. The article describes McInnes as a 'well-known progressive baker and confectioner' who made the move in order to cope with his growing business. It provides interesting detail about the premises:

> *While baking operations went on uninterruptedly at the old site, all preparations were being made at the new place for the setting up of a shop, bakehouse, plant, and all accessories on the most modern lines. The new premises have been enlarged and all facilities have been provided for the successful conduct of an up-to-date bakery establishment. The shop and bakehouse are liberally lighted with electricity, and electric power is also provided for the running of a capacious cake-making machine. Generally, every effort has been put forth to bring the bakery into conformity with the provisions of the Health Act.*[100]

Three years later, in 1921, McInnes placed an advertisement[101] calling for quotes to build a house and remove a bakery building. While this suggests that the relocated business may not have gone as well as he had hoped and while no information about the sale of the business or bakery has been located, by 1923, Cecil Smith Ward's 'Ideal Bakery' was operating on the Palmerin St site, with Ward later (1932) absorbing the 'Imperial Bakery' business of Edward Roffey Mitchell and employing him, as well as a business partner to coordinate deliveries.

In April 1934, Ward disposed of the business to a Mr Edward ('Ted') Mulhall 'late of Sydney'. It appears that Mulhall came to Warwick because he had been appointed conductor of the Warwick Town Band. He had been one of 20 applicants for the position and began work as soon as he arrived on 8 March 1934, preparing the band for their first concert under his direction just a fortnight later. Mulhall came with a reputation as a champion cornet player, teacher and conductor in Ayr and Mackay as well as in Sydney, but as he does not appear to have been a baker, the business may have been purchased as an investment.

Whether or not this was the case, Mulhall was the owner of the business for only a very brief time, selling it in early 1935 to Victor Elsley who had sold a seven-year lease

BUSINESS ARRANGEMENT

As intimated in the advertising columns of this issue, Mr. C. S. Ward, who has successfully carried on business as a baker and pastry cook for almost nine years at the Ideal Bakery, Palmerin-street, has now taken Mr. Emil Andersen into his business. From now on Mr. Andersen will be in charge of the distributing part of the firm's activities, while Mr. Ward will be able to devote the whole of his time to the supervision of the inside work, and the firm will carry on under the old trading name.

MON 26 SEP 1932. P2.

Another Business Announcement

We now wish to notify the people of Warwick and District that we have taken over Mitchell's Imperial Bakery Business, and that we have secured the services of Mr. C. R. Mitchell in our Bakery as from October 1st.
Also that these added facilities will enable us to specialise in an early delivery of bread for breakfast, school, and work lunches. Customers wishing to avail themselves of this early service are requested to please communicate with us. We guarantee to do the rest.

WARD'S IDEAL BAKERY
BAKERS ——— PASTRYCOOKS
Palmerin-street. 'Phone No. 132.

FRI 30 SEP 1932.

BAKERY BUSINESS SALE

Messrs. McCahon and Co., auctioneers, report having sold the lease, together with the stock and plant, of Mr. C. S. Ward's bakery business, in Palmerin-street, to Mr. E. Mulhall, late of Sydney, who will take over and conduct the business from 30th instant.

SAT 21 APR 1934. P6.

of the Palace Hotel in December the previous year. *The Courier-Mail* reported that 'following a holiday in Sydney, it is the intention of Mr Elsley to return to Warwick and commence in another class of business'.[102] That other 'class of business' was evidently baking because Elsley then constructed the new bakery, shop and living quarters which still stood in 2021, bearing his name and the year (1935) on the façade.

When the high cost of constructing the new premises led to financial difficulties for Elsley, he sold the business and leased the premises in November 1937 to Herbert George Glasby[103] who had previously owned or leased bakeries in several towns on the Downs (Oakey, Mitchell, Goondiwindi). However, by March 1938, barely four months later, Glasby had disposed of the lease and established a bakery in Chinchilla. Shortly afterwards, in September of that year, he was killed in a car accident, aged just 40.[w]

Later that year, Elsleys was purchased by Fred Parker (p. 78) and it was he who baked the first loaf in its bakehouse. The property would remain in the Parker family for over 35 years.

The bakery and shop ceased operating in the mid-1970s, becoming the offices of a legal firm in the early 1980s and being acquired by the Total Health and Education Foundation (formerly the Helen Vale Foundation).[104] Fred Parker had hoped to continue to live above the bakery in Palmerin St as he aged, but this did not prove possible.

In 2020, the buildings served as the offices of Osborn Consulting Engineers Pty Ltd.

---

w   Herbert George Clarke was not associated with Clarke and Glasby, the bakery business which operated at 58 Grafton St from 1939 until the 1950s.

Elsleys, September 2020. (Author's photograph.)

Side view and window detail, Elsleys, September 2020. (Author's photographs.)

58 Grafton Street

SUCCESSION

-1905.................. John Murray

1910.................... John David Askin

1916.................... Henry Reading

1935.................... Otto Meyer

1939.................... Harold Gordon Clarke

For the first half of the twentieth century, there were two bakeries operating in Grafton St – one at no. 76 (p. 158), and this one, a block further east at no. 58.

The first mention found of a bakery at this location is in newspaper reports of land auctions in Grafton St in late 1905 – 'one acre in the same street, on which are erected Mr Murray's bakery and five cottages'.

In July 1910, Murray sold his business to Moree merchant, John David Askin,[105] and his baker wife, Addie Kate (née Gall).

Askin launched his new business by posting a series of tiny advertisements on the same page of the *Warwick Examiner and Times* on 1 August, and continued this practice, progressively promoting the full range of his products and services – 'London pies', 'superior' pastry, catering, wedding cakes which are 'works of art', and especially his 'Malto-Pepsin' bread ('highly recommended by the medical faculty'). Within four months his business appears to have done well because advertisements referred to 'Askin and Co.' and had more than doubled in size.

Murray, meanwhile, had left the baking trade to try his hand as the licensee of The Australian Hotel. However, within three years, he was back in the trade, this time as the

Public Notice

THE undersigned in thanking the Public of Warwick and District for past support, notifies that he has disposed of his Bakery Business in Grafton-street to G. D. ASKIN, late of Moree, and hopes his old Customers will continue their support to the new proprietor.

JOHN MURRAY.

The undersigned wishes to inform the Public that he has taken over Mr. John Murray's business as from 1st April, and hopes by strict attention to business to merit a fair share of public support.

G. D. ASKIN.

WED 27 JUL 1910. P6.

owner/proprietor of the bakery at 76 Grafton St as well as the café formerly owned by David Webster in Palmerin St.

In August 1911, Askin was still advertising his 'Malto-Pepsin Bread' and by then had also applied his succinct advertising style to recruitment. However, at this point, the Askins lost their only child, eight-year-old Clifton Gall Askin. After Clifton's death and burial in the Warwick cemetery, the Askins moved to Toowoomba where he set up business as a cordial manufacturer before enlisting in the Australian Army in 1914. He served in Britain in the postal and pay corps throughout the War and, on return to Australia and discharge in 1920, he and Kate settled in NSW. He died in Gosford in 1930, at the age of 49.

Clifton Askin's gravestone, Warwick Cemetery.
(Photograph courtesy of Eric Turner.)

The trail at 58 Grafton St disappears from the Askins' departure in 1912 until Henry Reading's purchase of the business in 1916.

Reading had operated the bakery at 41 Albion St in 1908, but sold up and moved to Pratten in 1910 (p. 146). After six years, he returned to Warwick and was mentioned in association with a succession of locations, including 58 Grafton St. By 1932, he was no longer listed in the Electoral Rolls as a baker, appearing instead as a car driver, but he maintained ownership of the bakery.

In November 1935, Otto J. Meyer purchased the business from Henry Reading and operated it until 1939 when he moved from Warwick to the Western Queensland town of Texas.

Murwillumbah baker, Harold Gordon Clarke, then operated the bakery from 1939, forming a partnership, Clarke and Glasby. Details of the business are scant, but it is mentioned from 1947 to 1954 in such things as newspaper reports of Warwick show results, fines imposed for early baking (a regular transgression by all bakers), and the delivery schedules adopted by the local master bakers who were members of the Bread Manufacturers' Association.

During Clarke's tenure, Henry Reading took up a position as a cook, living and working at Scots College where he died suddenly in May 1948, aged 73.

As Reading still owned the bakery at the time of his death, the title transferred to his wife, Mary Jane. (Application for Transmission of Land Title for Section 30, Allotment 12, Sub-section 3, Re-sub 1. See Map below).

The date when the bakery finally closed is not known, but it appears that it would certainly have ceased operation in 1959 with Clarke's death (see p. 65).

Despite ceasing to operate as a bakery, the shop (with a new frontage) was still standing in 2020, owned and used by Jason Benz of Warwick Panel and Paint Works next door.

Sudden Death Of Cook At Scots College

Four hours after complaining that he felt ill, Henry Reading, 73, cook at The Scots' College, was found dead on his bed by the Principal (Mr J. A. Dunning) yesterday morning.

Reading had been cook at The Scots' College since February, 1942. He had been in indifferent health for some time, having spent a short period in hospital last February.

At 4.30 am yesterday he got up and went over to the college kitchen to attend to his duties, and at about 5 am complained to his assistant that he felt ill. He then went over to his room to lie down.

Shortly before 9 am, Mr Dunning called to inquire as to his condition and found that he apparently was dead. Mr Dunning informed the matron, who examined Reading and then summoned a doctor, who pronounced life extinct.

Police said yesterday the death was due to natural causes.

Reading leaves a widow, a daughter, Mrs C. Bloomfield, of Canning street, and a son, Mr H. H. Reading, of Hamilton street, East Warwick.

He resided in Canning street and was well known in Warwick, having operated bakeries in Albion, Fitzroy and Grafton streets in former years.

20 MAY 1948. P2.

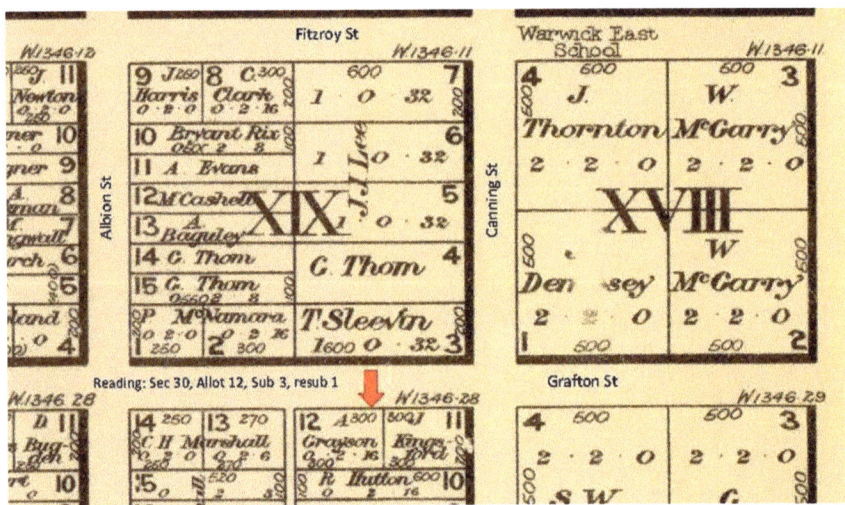

Location of Reading's property as per application for transmission of land title, July 1949. Map from plan of Warwick, 1879. (See Endnote 4.)

Image capture: March 2010 © Google Australia.

Photograph courtesy of Eric Turner (November 2020).

76 Grafton Street

SUCCESSION

Early 1900s ...... David Webster

1913 .... John Murray

1919 .... David Anderson Bremner and Albert Edward Bugden

c. 1923 .... James West

1925 .... Richard Emil Bochman

1931 .... Lloyd and Henry Crone

1961 .... Condamine Valley/Warwick Branch,
Queensland Country Women's Association

1966 .... building demolished

The Grafton St bakery most Warwick residents still recall is that which stood at 76 Grafton St, next to the Bochman Buildings, until 1966.

The person who first built and owned the bakery is not known, but the newspaper report of the sale to John Murray in August 1913 (right) records that David Webster had carried on business there 'for some years past' and the style of the building suggests that it was constructed early in the twentieth century.

Six years later, in September 1919, Murray sold the business to David Anderson Bremner and Albert Edward Bugden (p. 159).

As advertisements for Bremner and Bugden were published only until late 1923, it appears that they may

BUSINESS CHANGE.

The well-known tea rooms and bakery business in Warwick, which have been carried on by David Webster for some years past, have been purchased by Mr. John Murray, late of the Australian Hotel. An announcement to this effect appears in our advertising columns, and Mr. Murray took over the business yesterday. Before becoming licensee of the Australian Hotel, Mr. Murray had engaged in the baking business in Warwick and Stanthorpe, and has had a long experience in the trade. Patrons may therefore rely upon securing ready attention, and will be well catered for. A competent staff will be employed. Mrs. Murray will have charge of the Cafe, while the bakery business will be under the personal supervision of Mr. Murray himself. The services of Mr. King, of the Exchenhagen Cafe, Brisbane, have been secured, and he will take charge of the cake department.

SAT 2 AUG 1913. WET

then have sold it to James West because, on 3 February 1925, the advertisement below announced the transfer to Richard Bochman.

Richard Emil Bochman (p. 42) operated the bakery until 1931 when he leased it to the Crone brothers, Lloyd and 'Harry', who continued to operate it until the late 1950s (p. 67).

In 1961, the bakehouse, with its shop and upstairs flat, was acquired by the Condamine Valley/Warwick Branch of the Queensland Country Women's Association and renovated for use as a Rest Room.

The refurbished building opened in 1961, but after consultation with members, the Association decided to have the building demolished and to call tenders for construction of new, brick Rest Rooms. The building was constructed by Reg Roulston at a cost of $19,000 and officially opened in October 1966.

The newspaper report accompanying the photograph of the demolition noted that the Condamine Valley members occupied temporary quarters in the Bochman Buildings during construction and that, apart from rest and reception rooms, the new building would have 'a room 20 ft x 70 ft suitable for meetings and catering for wedding receptions'.

PUBLIC NOTICE.

MESSRS. BREMNER & BUDGEN have taken over the BAKERY BUSINESS in Grafton-street hitherto carried on by Mr. John Murray. Mr. Bremner has been for six years a Pastrycook with Mr. John Murray, while Mr. Budgen has been foreman baker with Mr. Jas. Callaghan for six years. The Business will be conducted on the same efficient lines as before, and the new master bakers solicit the same generous support as was bestowed on their predecessor.   185

THU 11 SEP 1919. P8.

NOTICE.

MR. JAMES WEST wishes to notify his debtors that he sold his business and all debts owing to him must be paid at the bakery in Grafton-street, before 28th February.   188

NOTICE.

MR. JAMES WEST begs to notify his numerous customers that he has disposed of his bakery business to Mr. R. BOCHMEN. He thanks his customers for their past favours and hopes that the same patronage which has been shown him will be accorded his successor.   189

NOTICE.

MR. R. BOCHMEN wishes to notify the people of Warwick and district that he has taken over the business lately carried on by Mr. James West and hopes for a fair share of patronage.   190

TUES 3 FEB 1925.

Newspaper clippings preserved by the Condamine Valley/Warwick Branch of the QCWA record the final stages of the life of the bakery. (Both photographs by John Harrison.)

Condamine Valley/Warwick Branch Rest Room, September 2020. (Author's photograph.)

Cnr Percy Street and Oak Avenue

SUCCESSION

1932................... Stanley Cain and Alfred Thorne

ex 1942.............. unknown

1958................... Mervyn and Alice Lancaster (Lancaster's Butchery)

ex 2006.............. unknown

2020................... Darling Downs Snacks

The shop and brick bakehouse on the corner of Percy St and Oak Ave were built in 1932 by Stan Cain.

Although Stan was aged only 19 at that time and barely out of his apprenticeship, his cabinetmaker father, Edward, and his mother Mary (née Munro) made the land and funds available for him to build the bakehouse and shop adjacent to the Cain family home at 61 Percy St. This was the second example of the generosity of the Cains towards their two sons, George and Stan (they had previously supported George to become a pharmacist).

For the years between the bakery's construction and March 1937, when title was transferred to the brothers, the Cain and Thorne business paid a weekly rental of £2 and the bakery continued to operate as Cain and Thorne until 1942 when the business was closed.

While information about the next 16 years is scant, accounts from Warwick residents suggest that the bakehouse and shop stood unused until some point in the 1950s when the bakehouse, shop and house at 61 Percy St were sold to the Canavans, a family of farmers from the Sladevale/Freestone area, north of Warwick. It is known that the house at some point was divided into two flats and that Percy Canavan operated a butchery business from the shop, supplied with meat from the slaughter yard on the Canavan family farm.

Mervyn Brian Lancaster, and his wife Alice (née Monahan) arrived in Warwick from Nobby in 1958 and initially rented the house and shop from the Canavans before purchasing both properties from them in the 1960s.

According to Electoral Rolls and personal communications from Warwick residents and members of the Lancaster family, Merv. and Alice operated the butcher shop until c. 1968. When it closed, the Lancaster family used the shop as a storage shed. After Merv's death in 1995 at the age of 66, Alice continued to live on her own at 61 Percy St until she died in October 2006, aged 81. Both house and shop were then sold in June/July 2007.

Photographs taken by Cain and McFarlane family descendants in March 2008 show both shop and house in disrepair with only the remnants of the brick chimney and firebox where the bakehouse once stood and the faint registered number of the butcher shop (2779) on the façade as records of the building's 76-year past life.

However, the street view captured for Google Earth in March 2010 shows that both the shop and the house at 61 Percy St had been renovated by that year, and a photograph taken by Eric Turner in 2020 shows the smartly presented premises of Darling Downs Snacks.

A standard bag of flour weighed 150 lb – without the Cain family dog.
(Photograph courtesy of Janice Aldred.)

The original shop and house at 61 Percy St in March 2008.
(Photograph courtesy of Janice Aldred, daughter of Stanley Cain.)

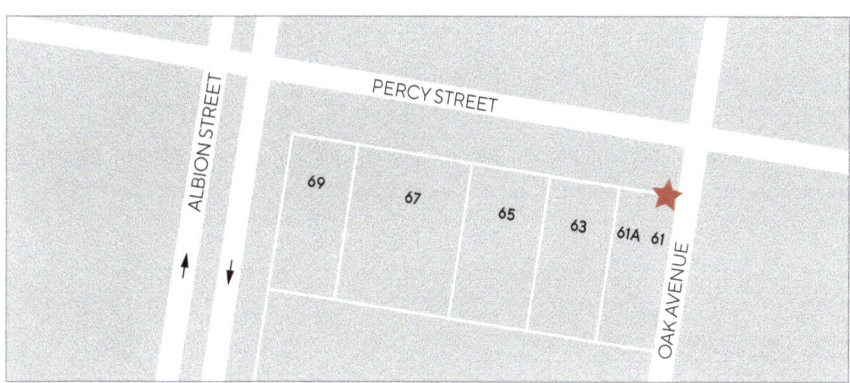

The shop number for Mervyn Lancaster's butcher shop was still clearly visible on the façade in 2008. (Photograph courtesy of Janice Aldred.)

The repainted house and renovated shop, available for lease.
Image capture: March 2010 © Google Australia.

Darling Downs Snacks, 2020. (Photograph courtesy of Eric Turner.)

Lex McFarlane, son of Warwick baker, 'Nev' McFarlane, at the bakehouse in March 2008. Image shows the remains of the chimney and outline of the firebox.
(Photograph courtesy of Janice Aldred.)

If bread is the staff of life,
what is the life of the staff?

One long loaf!

A 'Bluey and Curley' cartoon with this caption was tacked to the wall in Brown's Bakery for many years. The characters of Bluey and Curley were created by Alex Gurney. Born in England in 1902, Gurney came to Australia in 1937 and became a prolific cartoonist for newspapers in Australia, New Zealand and Canada. Readers followed the adventures of the two larrikin diggers through WWII and into post-war civilian life. After Gurney's death in 1955, his cartoon was continued by other artists for several more years. (Illustration from *Flood, Fire and Fever, A History of Elwood* by Meyer Eidelson, St Kilda Historical Society. No acknowledgement available.)

OUR DAILY BREAD

The advertisements below are for some of the early bakery businesses not elaborated elsewhere in this book, including a rare female baker and two competing co-operative enterprises. Like the other advertisements, they are snapshots in time. Approaches to advertising were different, as were the products once offered by bakers, but then, as now, there was a sense of pride, excitement and optimism as new businesses opened and new products were launched. And gossip was evidently as powerful then as it is in the age of the internet!

NOTICE! NOTICE!
NEW BAKERY,
PALMERIN-STREET, WARWICK.

MESSRS. POWER & HACKETT
BEG to inform their friends and the public of Warwick generally, that they intend starting in the above business on the

First Day of AUGUST Next,
And guarantee full weight for money. Their friends and the public generally may rely on getting a good article and regularity in serving.
Note the address—
POWER & HACKETT,
Bakers,
726   Back of Mr. Selkes', Palmerin-street.

SAT 8 SEP 1877. P3. WET

REMOVED! REMOVED!
E. T. ANDERSON
BEGS to inform her customers and the general public, that she has
REMOVED
To those premises lately occupied by MR. JAMES M'DOUGALL.

The Bakery Business
So successfully carried on by Mr. James M'Dougall for the last 12 years, will still be continued and conducted under experienced supervision.
All orders will receive prompt attention.
119   E. T. ANDERSON.

SAT 2 FEB 1878. P3. WET

**WARWICK
CO-OPERATIVE BAKERY,**
NEXT COSMOPOLITAN HOTEL.

GLOVER & HOLLOWAY,
Fancy Bread & Biscuit Bakers,
CONFECTIONERS, &c.   87

THU 7 FEB 1878. P3. WATG

NOTICE OF SALE.

I HAVE to inform my Customers and the Public generally that I have sold my Bakery Business to JAMES POMEROY, and while thanking my very numerous customers for the liberal support which they have tendered to me I trust that the same will be extended to my successor, whom I feel will by civility and promptness to business merit the best support of the public generally.

MICHAEL CARROLL.

In reference to the above, having purchased this business, I hope by strict attention to customers and by always turning out the best of articles to receive my full share of the patronage of the Public of Warwick.
Always a fresh supply of small goods on hand made from the very best materials. Wedding, and other Cakes made to order at the shortest notice.

JAMES POMEROY.

SAT 16 FEB 1907. P6. WET

NEW BAKERY.
CHEAP BREAD! CHEAP BREAD!

THE CO-OPERATIVE BAKING COMPANY have NOW COMMENCED BUSINESS, and they are prepared to Regularly Deliver BREAD on and after 1st JULY, at

3D. PER 2LB. LOAF.

ALL ORDERS PUNCTUALLY ATTENDED TO.

BAKERY—Albion-street, opposite the Lands Office.
                                    J. T. WALLACE,
585   Manager.

SAT 28 JUL 1888. P4. WA

It was rumored in Warwick yesterday that a steam bakery and biscuit factory will shortly be established in this town on a large scale.

SAT 8 JUL 1911. P4. WET

The men and women listed on the following pages owned, operated or worked in Warwick's bakeries as masters, bakers, pastrycooks, confectioners, apprentices and carters from the 1860s to the 1960s. The list is included as a tribute to the many individuals who ensured that the people of Warwick and district received their daily bread. My thanks go to Michael Carter who generously created a database to capture the information.

While some 160 names have been gleaned from electoral rolls, business directories, newspapers, books and family stories, the list is by no means exhaustive and, in some cases, time has erased all but a passing reference. 'Fred' is one such example, defined in a 1926 newspaper story only as the German who 'had a bakery which Mr John Healy afterwards took over'.[106]

Emil Anderson
Mrs E.T. Anderson
John David Askin
William Benner Blackburn
Richard Emil Bochman
David Anderson Bremner
William Brennan
Athol Beresford ('Jim') Bright
William Brown
Martin Ralph Brown
Ralph Ashley Brown
Albert Edward Budgen
Michael Richard Buggie
Burnett
John Butler
Henry John ('Harry') Byrnes
James Callaghan
Stanley Alex Munro Cain
John Cameron
Michael Carroll
William John Carter
Michael Carter
Margaret Carter
Alex Cathro
Charlotte Clark
'Jim' Clark
Harold Gordon Clarke
Charles Henry Clarke
Clarence Edward Clarke
Celestino Gobbi Clarkeo
John Jefferson Paul Clarke
Henry Alexander Conley
George Alfred Cook
John Cooke
A.W.D. Cox
Stanley Cox
John Henry ('Harry') Crone
Lloyd James Herbert Crone
William Cunningham

Alfred Dempster
Mark Devine
Colin Donaldson
Leslie Allan ('Don') Donaldson
Daphne Blanche Donaldson
Jan Davidowicz
Charles G. Downes
H.E. Downes
Victor Emanuel Elsley
Callaghan Foote
Lyla French
Rex French
William Bede Gates
Charles Gilm
Herbert George Glasby
Glover
Albert ('Bert') Goodwin
Gorman
George Grant
Daniel Grigg
Frederick William Gottlieb Groth
R. Hackett
Joseph Vincent Hall
Mary Alexius Hall
Jack Hart
James Thomas Head
John Healy
S. Heather
Lionel Herbert
Kevin Hohenhaus
Brendan Holland
Clarence ('Clarrie') Hollingsworth
Holloway
Michael Horne
Benjamin Ingham
George Jones
Arthur John Kelly
George A. Keong
G.R. Kirkup

Robert Lamb
Joseph Lane
'Bert' Lawrence
Francis Thomas Lawrence
T.W. Lawrence
Clarence Edward Locke
James ('Sid') Lowe
Neville Matthews
Daniel Maunsell
Otto Joseph Meyer
J. McCabe & Co.
James McDougall
William Neville McFarlane
David Sutherland McGregor
Godfrey Bernard McInnes
West Hamilton McQuaker
Kevin Mellon
Neville Mills
C.R. Mitchell
Edward Roffey Mitchell
Owen Leslie Mollenhauer
Margaret Mary Mollenhauer
Arthur Ernest Morris
Mervyn Arthur Mouritz
Edward Mulhall
John Murray
A. Myers
Samuel Lindesay Neil
'Bernie' Nielsen
John Newby
Augustus John Lawson Newton
David George Newton
William George Newton
James Noyes
John Patrick O'Mara
Louis Ellingson Overstead
Leslie Elliott Overstead
Gordon Elliott Overstead
Frederick Charles Parker

Jack Frederick Parker
Mervyn Stan Parker
Ellen Pavey
James Pomeroy
Power
William ('Bill') Rach
Henry Reading
Francis ('Frank') Reeves
William Riddle
N.T. Rose
J.P. Ross
Alexander Herbert Ross
Charles Henry Rowe
W. Rutledge
Tom Ryan
Roger Thomas McArthur Schmidt
Alfred Victor Scott
Neville Scott
Jack J. Sheeran
Trevor Sheeran
Lancelot ('Lance') Shelley
Wallace William Siebuhr
Patrick Slattery
Albert Southworth
Douglas Neil ('Junior') Spinks
Arthur Steele
Brad Steele
Wayne Steele
Joseph Stockbridge
Mrs Stockbridge
William Edward Strudwick
'Bernie' Surawski
Leonard Sweeney
Thompson
Alfred Thorne
Fred Tanna
Henry Tucker
Norman Richings Tucker
Alfred Richings Tucker

Leonard Charles Cyril Tucker
J.T. Wallace
Cecil Smith Ward
James West
Stanley Warne
Joseph White

Graham Wiedman
Henry August Willersdorf
Mervyn Willet
Allan Gilmour Winchester
Fred

Parker's Bakery calendar (1939) with Fred Parker in front of the Harvey oven in his bakery at 148 Palmerin St. (Calendar given to Michael Carter by Fred Parker c. 1977. Photograph courtesy of Michael Carter.)

REFLECTIONS

In the 1950s, there were six bakeries operating in Warwick; in 2020 there were just three independent enterprises: Steele's Bakery and Café at 55 Fitzroy St, Westside Hotbread at 146 Wood St, and the Ranch Bakehouse at 20 Wood St.

Few memories and traditions of the trade in the 20th century remain and even fewer physical traces survive of the bakeries that supplied the town with its daily bread during its first century. Since the 1960s and early 1970s, bakehouses have been demolished, baking families have moved away, and it's difficult to imagine any contemporary bakery reporting, as the Tucker family proudly did in 1951, that more than 20 million loaves had passed through their King St ovens in 37 years.[107]

The three bakeries that operated in Warwick at the time this book was written typify the changes seen throughout Australia in the baking trade in the last half-century – and the speed of that change. A baker no longer needs the physical strength to lift a 150 lb bag of flour or the stamina to work long, inconvenient hours to produce fresh bread each morning; he no longer needs to know how to make his own yeast; and he no longer has to deal with the large and temperamental wood- and gas-fired ovens – or unpredictable horses.

In the 21st century, women are more likely to enter the trade; advances in engineering and bread science have enabled bakers to produce a consistent product; and electric ovens are compact, reliable and efficient.

But has something been lost in the process?

The emergence of plant bakeries and mass-produced bread, as well as the development of quick and highly efficient transport and logistics, means that the baker in 2021 is no longer the familiar local person who delivers bread to the back door. The eponymous bakeries such as Bochman's, Tucker's, Parker's, Brown's, Crone's, Reading's, Cain's, etc. in Warwick, have been replaced almost completely by business names and brands, invented to suggest freshness, taste, and the comforts of home or an imagined rural idyll. Because the baker has become anonymous, customer choice is driven by factors such as cost, convenience and the impact of marketing, rather than by customer loyalty.

Further, the 21st century has seen the spread of baking franchises, the emergence of bakeries within supermarkets, and the development of bench-top bread machines for the home. When combined with the normal vagaries of the marketplace and a more mobile population, these developments mean that bakeries need to be agile and adapt constantly to survive. Such an environment tends to tip the scales against the collaborative, mutually supportive family enterprises of old.

But there is a 'plus' side to this ledger.

'Old school' bakers like my father and grandfather decried the quality, keeping ability and taste of mass-produced bread and would be delighted to see the emergence, this century, of artisanal bakeries producing products such as authentic sourdough. They would be equally pleased to see the concomitant growth of understanding that, while good bread is indeed about the baker, his technique and his oven, it is also about ingredients – they could never have imagined that wheat farmers and flour millers would one day produce single-origin flour, as carefully monitored and controlled as any Scotch whisky.

As the child of a baking family, I am both part of this history and its historian. My hope is that the lives I have discovered and the stories, memories and traditions people have so generously shared with me will contribute to the bigger picture of Warwick's past, and produce greater community awareness of the role of the baking trade in the town's history.

I also hope that people will continue to rediscover the pleasures of one of the world's oldest foods – bread. At its simplest, it may be just a random combination of flour, salt, yeast and water, but what a sublime combination it is. Cervantes was right; 'all sorrows are less with bread'.[108]

RECOMMENDED READING AND RESOURCES

Three particular writers have made valuable contributions to recording the local history of Warwick.

Thomas Hall collaborated with S.P. Fletcher in the 1890s to publish an illustrated book *Floss, or the progress of an adventurer in the regions of Australia*, and in 1903 recorded his extensive knowledge of the local Aborigines in *A short History of the Downs blacks known as The Blucher Tribe*. However, the work for which he is best known and remembered is *The early history of Warwick district and pioneers of the Darling Downs*. First published in 1920, seven further editions or print runs were published. An electronic version of the 1925 edition of his Warwick history can be downloaded free of charge from The University of Queensland's eSpace.

Hall was born in Aberdeen, Scotland, in 1844. Together with his parents and siblings, he migrated to Queensland in 1853 and travelled to Canning Downs by horse and dray. He and his three brothers all became expert bushmen and Hall himself became a skilled farmer, working for many years on properties in the Warwick district.

Hall and Jane Tulloch were married at Swan Creek in March 1875 and went on to have 11 children. At the time of their Golden Anniversary in 1925, they had 23 grandchildren and many Hall descendants still live on the Darling Downs. He died suddenly in June 1928 at the age of 83.

Sudden Deaths

TWO WARWICK RESIDENTS

SAD HAPPENING

Within about three hours of receipt of the news of the sudden death of Mr. Thomas Hall yesterday morning, Mrs. John A. Stewart, a niece, collapsed at the telephone, and died shortly afterwards. The tragic happening caused a shock throughout the whole of the Warwick district, great sympathy being felt for the sorrowing relatives. The Town Hall flag was flown at half-mast. The late Mr. Hall bore his 83 years remarkably well, and appeared to be in the best of health up to the time of his demise, which occurred with pathetic suddenness in a paddock adjoining his home. Always an early riser, Mr. Hall had prepared the feed for his pony shortly after 7.30 o'clock. While leading the animal from an adjoining paddock, with the bridle under his arm, he was seen to stagger and collapse at the gate. He died in the arms of his wife and a neighbour without regaining consciousness. Always of a cheery and lovable disposition, Mr. Hall had been heard singing while getting the feed ready for the pony.

SAT 30 JUN 1928.

Joseph Simon McKey developed a strong interest in local history and wrote five books: *The Warwick Story* (1972), *Dawn Over the Darling Downs* (1977), *The Light of Other Days* (1978), *Linger Longer* (1979), and *Wattle Scented Warwick* (1982).

McKey was born in Warwick in 1904 and attended local schools before working on his father's farm and in a local cheese factory. He played football and trained as a boxer but at the age of 19 decided to join the priesthood. Ordained in Warwick in 1934, he served in various locations before contracting tuberculosis and, four years later, settling permanently in Warwick.

He was never well enough to assume full parish responsibilities, but worked as a dental mechanic, learned to repair clocks and watches, built several telescopes as an amateur astronomer, learned to fly, built and operated motor boats, and built five seismographs to make recordings of earthquakes and other disturbances. He was also a keen photographer and painter, and, to strengthen his lungs, learned to play the bagpipes and joined the Warwick Thistle Band.

He died in 1982 and is buried in the Warwick cemetery.

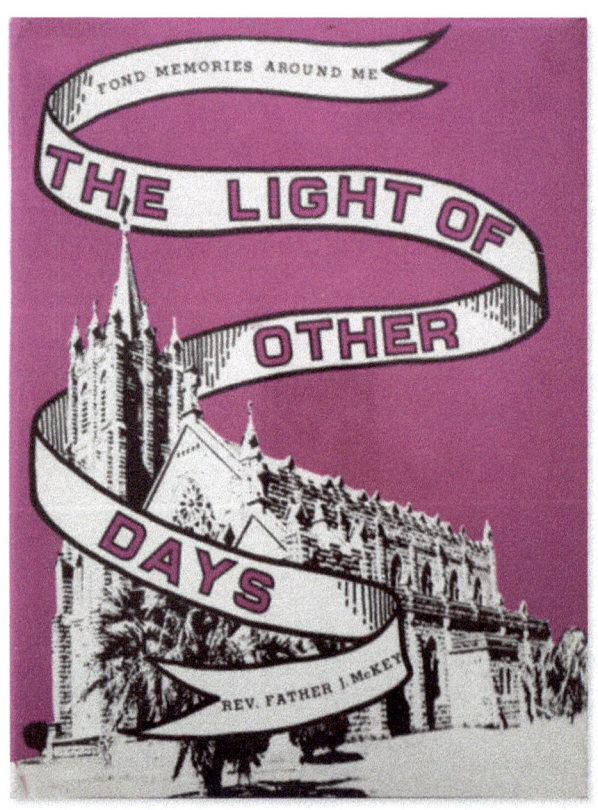

Donald McInnes produced more than 250 newspaper columns about the history of Warwick and the surrounding districts. Written under the pen-name 'Gooragooby, Dalveen', his columns were published as 'Echoes of the Past' in the *Warwick Daily News* between 1926 and 1943 and are regarded as an authentic record. Copies of his columns can be found through Trove (see p. 178).

McInnes's grandparents had arrived with the first pioneer settlers, and his father was the first white child born on the Darling Downs (6 January 1843). Donald himself was born on 18 June 1868 and, after completing his education at local schools, began a career in journalism, working for the *Warwick Examiner and Times* for eight years, and for a further two years at the *Warwick Argus*. He then joined the Queensland Railway Department and, until his retirement in the 1930s, served as stationmaster at a number of stations in southern Queensland, including 25 years at the Granite Belt settlement of Dalveen.

He was keenly interested in cricket, but his abiding passion was local history. As a tribute to his contribution, the committee for the Darling Downs Centenary Celebrations chose him to lead the commemorative procession through Warwick representing Allan Cunningham, the explorer and botanist who had been the first European to see the Downs in 1837, naming the region after Sir Ralph Darling, the then Governor of New South Wales.

When McInnes died in August 1943, the *Warwick Daily News* published a generous tribute written by his fellow columnist 'Boomerang'.[109] It included this reference to his role in the centenary procession: 'Mounted on a bay charger, he portrayed the part admirably as he led the procession through gaily decorated streets thronged with thousands of spectators. This procession was freely acclaimed as the best ever witnessed in Warwick'.

The portrait above was published in the centenary souvenir booklet to which he contributed.

Other recommended resources

Parsons, David (2003), *Wadingh A History of Aboriginal People in the Warwick Area and Their Land,* Toowoomba: self-published. (Available free of charge to download as a University of Southern Queensland eprint.)

Trove (This Australian online library database includes full text documents and digital images and is a collaboration between the National Library of Australia and hundreds of partner organisations around Australia. It can be accessed through the National Library of Australia website.)

Warwick and District Historical Society, 81/83 Dragon St, Warwick 4370. (The Society was formed in 1966 and has operated the Pringle Cottage museum since 1968. In addition to its valuable collection of objects and ephemera which is open to the public, the society has volunteer researchers who can assist with enquiries.)

Waterman, D.B. (1967), *Squatter, Selector, and Storekeeper: a history of the Darling Downs 1859-93,* Sydney: Sydney University Press.

ENDNOTES AND REFERENCES

1. Farrer, K.T.H. (1988). Food Technology. In Australian Academy of Technological Sciences and Engineering, *Technology in Australia 1788-1988: A condensed history of Australian technological innovation and adaptation during the first two hundred years*, (pp. 72-73 and 96-97). Melbourne: Australian Academy of Technological Sciences and Engineering.
2. Gerler, C.F., Map of Brisbane (1844). In Barton E.J.T. (Ed.) (1909). *Jubilee history of Queensland* (p. 12). Brisbane: H.J. Diddams and Co.)
3. Queensland State Archives image licensed under CC BY 4.0.
4. Queensland. Department of Lands, Survey Branch (1879). *Plan of the town of Warwick, Parish of Warwick, County of Merivale, District of Darling Downs*, Queensland. Brisbane: Survey Branch, Lands Department, Queensland.
5. Hall, T. (1925). *The early history of Warwick district and pioneers of the Darling Downs* (p. 77). Toowoomba: Robertson and Provan.
6. Non-British migrants to the Australian colonies did not have the same rights and privileges as British settlers until 1849 when 'naturalisation' was introduced, giving them most of the same rights, including the right to own land.

    Under the *Naturalization Act of 1903*, a person resident in the Commonwealth who was not a British subject or 'aboriginal native of Asia, Africa, or the Islands of the Pacific, excepting New Zealand' could apply to the Governor General for a *Certificate of Naturalization* if they intended to settle in the Commonwealth and had resided in Australia continuously for two years immediately preceding the application. (NSW archives.)
7. McInnes, D. (1934, 29 September). Echoes of the past: Genesis of Stanthorpe. *Warwick Daily News*, p. 7.
8. *Warwick Argus and Tenterfield Chronicle* (1872, 27 July), p. 3.
9. NSW Registry of Births Deaths and Marriages, registration no. 2171/1866.
10. McInnes, D. (1937, 24 April). Echoes of the past: Lost in the city's main street. *Warwick Daily News*, p. 3.
11. Bureau of Meteorology (September 2019). *Flood Warning System for the Condamine River to Warwick*. Australian Government.
12. *Warwick Examiner and Times* (1890, 12 March), p. 2.
13. *Warwick Examiner and Times* (1890, 12 March), p. 2.
14. *Warwick Examiner and Times* (1900, 20 January), p. 7.
15. Queensland State Archives record the following sequence of local government entities in Warwick

Warwick Municipal Council	25 May 1861	to 31 March 1903
Warwick Town Council	31 March 1903	to 2 April 1936
Warwick City Council	4 April 1936	to 15 July 1994
Warwick Shire Council	1 July 1994	to 15 March 2008
Southern Down Regional Council	15 March 2008	to present

16. *Warwick Examiner and Times* (1884, 15 March), p. 3.
17. McInnes, D. (1936, 23 June). Echoes of the past: Early day Chinese. *Warwick Daily News*, p. 3.
18. Queensland State Archives Digital Image collection – ID 1098212.
19. Queensland State Archives Digital Image collection – ID 1098218, oath 896a.
20. *Warwick Argus and Tenterfield Chronicle* (1866, 14 March), p. 2.
21. Winterbotham, J. – Find a Grave ID 48166878 (2016). *Find a Grave* Memorial 171985486.
22. *The Queenslander* (1871, 22 April), p. 3.
23. *Queensland Times, Ipswich Herald and General Advertiser* (1875, 4 December), p. 5.
24. *Warwick Examiner and Times* (1881, 14 September), p. 2.
25. *Toowoomba Chronicle and Darling Downs General Advertiser* (1893, 25 February, p. 4.
26. *Warwick Examiner and Times* (1901, 2 February), p. 2.
27. *Warwick Examiner and Times* (1898, 19 February), p. 7.
28. *Warwick Examiner and Times* (1904, 17 February), p. 5.
29. *Warwick Examiner and Times* (1873, 3 May), p. 3.
30. *Warwick Examiner and Times* (1873, 15 November), Family Notices, p. 2.
31. *Warwick Examiner and Times* (1874, 7 February), p. 2.
32. *Warwick Examiner and Times* (1874, 18 July), p. 2.
33. *Warwick Examiner and Times* (1874, 15 August), p. 2.

34 *Warwick Examiner and Times* (1874, 19 September), p. 4.
35 *Warwick Examiner and Times* (1885, 2 May), p. 3.
36 See Endnote 4.
37 Schneeleopard, J. (25 September 2014). Burg Kriebstein über dem Zschopautal. Creative Commons Attribution-Share Alike 3.0 Germany.
38 *Warwick Daily News* (1936, 3 March). Advertisement, p. 6.
39 *Warwick Daily News* (1932, 1 October), p. 8.
40 *Warwick Daily News* (1933, 25 November), p. 8.
41 *Warwick Daily News* (1934, 30 November), p. 8.
42 *Warwick Daily News* (1936, 24 March), p. 2.
43 *Warwick Daily News* (1936, 9 March), p. 6.
44 *Warwick Daily News* (1936, 15 September), p. 3.
45 *Warwick Daily News* (1937, 1 May), p. 2.
46 *Warwick Daily News* (1944, 24 March), p. 2.
47 *Warwick Daily News* (1940, 11 January), p. 8.
48 *Warwick Daily News* (1941, 18 October). Who's Who in Warwick advertising supplement, p. 12.
49 *Warwick Daily News* (1938, 5 August), p. 8.
50 *The Courier-Mail* (1954, 26 November), p. 10.
51 *Warwick Daily News* (1936, 9 June), p. 8.
52 *Warwick Daily News* (1928, 28 July). Obituary – Mr Dan Maunsell, p. 3.
53 *Warwick Argus* (1887, 8 April). Warwick Police Court, p. 3
54 *Warwick Examiner and Times* (1898, 30 November), p. 3.
55 *Warwick Examiner and Times* (1918, 23 March), p. 3.
56 *Warwick Examiner and Times* (1918, 28 September). Property and Other Sales, p. 1.
57 *Warwick Daily News* (1926, 28 October). Bread Exhibition, p. 4.
58 *Warwick Daily News* (1928, 28 July). Obituary – Mr Dan Maunsell, p. 3.
59 *Warwick Daily News* (1928, 17 August), p. 8.
60 *Warwick Daily News* (1928, 22 August), p. 8.
61 *Warwick Daily News* (1949, 13 October), p. 6.
62 *Warwick Daily News* (1935, 10 August). Mr E. Parker: Retirement from Business, p. 2.
63 *Catholic Advocate* (1927, 28 April), p. 13.
64 *Warwick Daily News* (1934, 2 February). Bakery Sale, p.13.
65 *Warwick Daily News* (1982, 4 February), Obituary – Fred Parker.
66 *Warwick Daily News* (1934, 18 July). Horse plunges into river, p. 4.
67 *Warwick Daily News* (1939, 1 July). Baker's Horse Bolts, p. 2.
68 *Warwick Daily News* (1947, 13 December), p. 10.
69 Giedion, S. (1948). *Mechanization Takes Command: A contribution to anonymous history*. New York: Oxford University Press.
70 Haden, R. (2006). Australian history in the baking: the rebirth of the Scotch oven. *Journal of Australian Studies*, 30:87, pp. 61-73.
71 Ibid. p. 65.
72 Ibid. pp. 71-72.
73 *Grenfell Record and Lachlan District Advertiser* (1908, 2 May), p. 7.
74 Timmy B (2012, March 25). Scotch oven restoration – part one 'Discovery' (Web log post). Retrieved from *Sourdough* 'a community of bakers from all over the world sharing a passion for great bread'.
75 Different strains of wheat have different levels of protein. This enables production of classes of flour with different levels of protein. Pastrycooks prefer lower protein classes whereas bread bakers prefer flour with a protein level of 11 or 12 per cent. Most Australian wheats were, and still are, low in protein by world standards, partly because of declining soil fertility, particularly nitrogen levels. (Shaw, P. (1988). Wheat protein – putting the N into protein, *Riverina Outlook Conference*.)
76 *Warwick Daily News* (1941, 18 October), p. 8.
77 *Glen Innes Examiner* (1942, 24 October), p. 2.
78 *Warwick Daily News* (1950, 23 December). "Bread Industry in Perilous Condition", p. 2.
79 *Warwick Daily News* (1944, 15 December). Release of 130 Bakers Sought, p. 1.
80 *Warwick Daily News* (1945, 16 January). Army to release 36 bakers, p. 3.

81 Casey and Lowe Pty Ltd Archaeology and Heritage (September 2002). History of Barker's Mill Darling Harbour. In *Report to CW-DC Pty Ltd on behalf of BHBB Pty Ltd*. Location: Author.
82 Refshauge, Richard (1969). Clark, Charles George (1832-1896). In *Australian Dictionary of Biography*, Vol.3. Location: Melbourne University Press.
83 Waterson, D.B., A Darling Downs Quartet – Four Minor Queensland Politicians: George Clark, James Morgan, William Allan and Francis Kates, pp. 1-4.
84 *The Brisbane Courier* (1876, 15 November), p. 5.
85 Valued at over $938,000 in 2020 according to the Reserve Bank of Australia's Pre-decimal Inflation Counter.
86 *The Brisbane Courier* (1912, 22 August), p. 7.
87 Costar, B.J. (1979). Barnes, George Powell (1856-1949). In *Australian Dictionary of Biography*, Vol.7. Location: Melbourne University Press.
88 Mark Baker Town Planning Consultant Pty Ltd in association with Ivan McDonald Architects (January 2010), Southern Downs Cultural Heritage Study Volume 1 – Main Report, p. 24.
89 Australian Trade Practices Tribunal Decision 40-012 (1976, 5 March). Re Queensland Co-operative Milling Association Ltd., Defiance Holdings Ltd. (proposed mergers with Barnes Milling Ltd.) Review of Commission's determination denying authorization.
90 *Lost Face of Warwick* (2020, 26 January). Renamed *Lost Faces of Warwick and District*, March 2021.
91 *Telegraph* (1873, 24 April), p. 2.
92 *Warwick Daily News* (1950, 27 October), p. 3.
93 The *Queensland Heritage Act* requires a Council to have and maintain a Local Heritage Register. The Southern Downs Register is a list of places considered to be of cultural heritage significance and includes details of the location and cultural heritage significance of each place.
94 *Warwick Daily News* (1940, 5 October). New Fruiterer, p. 7.
95 *Warwick Daily News* (1948, 28 December), p. 1.
96 *Sunshine Coast Daily* (2018, 7 January). How to tell if you're really a Warwick local.
97 *Warwick Daily News* (1943, 13 April). Obituary Mr W.B. Blackburn, p. 2.
98 The only known bakeries in Grafton St at this time were at no. 58 and no. 76. It is not known which bakery McInnes operated from.
99 *Warwick Examiner and Times* (1918, 23 January), p. 7.
100 *Warwick Examiner and Times* (1918, 16 January), p. 1.
101 *Warwick Daily News* (1921, 29 December), p. 6.
102 *The Courier-Mail* (1934, 1 December), p. 15.
103 *Warwick Daily News* (1937, 9 October), p. 6.
104 The Helen Vale Foundation (later renamed the Total Health and Education Foundation was established in Melbourne by Indian-born yoga teacher, the late Vijayadev Yogendra. It began as a voluntary association in 1970 and became a company limited by guarantee in 1975. In the early 1980s, Yogendra and more than 50 of his followers moved to Warwick from Melbourne and built a school and a collective of homes on Freestone Rd. The group's successful association with bakeries in Melbourne led to the construction of the Dome Bakery (Cafe Jacqui's in 2020) in Albion St in 1987 and may also have prompted the interest in Parker's Bakery.
105 *Warwick Daily News* (1910, 27 July), p. 6. The Public Notice lists him as G.D. Askin but this appears to be a typographical error.
106 *Warwick Daily News* (1926, 13 August). Warwick – Then and Now, p. 6.
107 *Warwick Daily News* (1951, 4 May), p. 2.
108 de Cervantes Saavedra, M. (1902). *The Life and Exploits of the Ingenious Gentleman Don Quixote De La Mancha*. London: Sand & Company. p. 530.
109 *Warwick Daily News* (1943, 22 September), p. 3.

About the author

For Judith Anderson as a child, fresh bread was the smell of morning.

Born into a family of bakers in Warwick on Queensland's Darling Downs, she lived for her first 18 years beside the Brown family bakery before pursuing higher education and a career which ranged from teaching, health education, and journalism to marketing, management and the performing arts. Now retired, she lives in Brisbane.

Back cover photos:

Top left: Daniel Maunsell, Baker and Confectioner, Warwick, c. 1900. (John Oxley Library, State Library of Queensland Neg. No: 102507.)

Top right: Stan Cain, baker. (Photograph courtesy of Janice Aldred.)

Bottom: Palmerin St, Warwick, on St George's Day, 23 April 1913. (Dornbusch family photograph from John Dean Collection, restored by Rolf Wood, courtesy of Máire Oakwood.)